Supercook's
Two + Two
COOKBOOK

ENIGMA

All weight and measure equivalents are approximate.
Tablespoons and teaspoons are Standard Spoon measures and are level.

For the purpose of recipe conversion, Standard British teaspoons and tablespoons are equivalent to Standard American ones.

Key to Symbols

☆ This is a guide to each recipe's preparation and cooking

☆ Easy

☆ ☆ Requires special care

☆ ☆ ☆ Complicated

① This is a guide to the cost of each dish and will, of course, vary according to region and season

① Inexpensive

① ① Reasonable

① ① ① Expensive

⧖ This is a guide to the preparation and cooking time required for each dish and will vary according to the skill of the individual cook

⧖ Less than 1 hour

⧖ ⧖ Between 1 hour and $2\frac{1}{2}$ hours

⧖ ⧖ ⧖ Over $2\frac{1}{2}$ hours

Dry Measures: Equivalents

British and American	Metric
1 oz.	28.3 grams (approx. 30 grams)
3 oz.	85 grams
1 lb. (16 oz.)	454 grams (approx. 500 grams or $\frac{1}{2}$ kg.)
35 oz. (2 lb. 3 oz.)	1000 grams or 1 kg.

Liquid Measures: Equivalents

British	American	Metric
$\frac{1}{6}$ fl. oz.	1 teaspoon	5 ml. approx.
$\frac{1}{2}$ fl. oz.	1 tablespoon	15 ml. approx.
1 fl. oz.	2 tablespoons	30 ml. approx.
8 fl. oz.	1 cup	2.27 dl.
10 fl. oz. ($\frac{1}{2}$ pint)	$1\frac{1}{4}$ cups	2.83 dl.
16 fl. oz.	1 pint (2 cups)	4.5 dl. or .45 litre approx. $\frac{1}{2}$ litre
20 fl. oz. (1 pint)	$2\frac{1}{2}$ cups	5.68 dl.
35 fl. oz. (2 lb. 3 oz.)	$4\frac{1}{3}$ cups	10 dl. or 1 litre

Linear Measures

1 inch	= 25 millimetres ($2\frac{1}{2}$ centimetres)
1 foot	= 300 millimetres (30 centimetres)
40 inches	= 1 metre (100 centimetres)

Readers Please Note:
Equivalents for American ingredients are given in the text in square brackets.

Recipes and food preparation by
Elaine Bastable, Isabel James, Jennie Reekie
Photography by Paul Kemp and John Lee
Illustrations by Jannat Houston

Published by Enigma Books,
58 Old Compton Street, London W1V 5PA
© Marshall Cavendish Limited 1973, 1974, 1977

This material was first published in
50 Super Meals for Friends and Family and
Cooking for Two

First printing 1974
Second Printing 1977

Printed in Hong Kong

ISBN 0 85685 051 9

ABOUT THIS BOOK

How many times have you had nothing in the kitchen to serve an unexpected guest or been unprepared for a special occasion or end-of-the-month budgeting? Or do you feel prevented from trying new recipes because you are only cooking for two? Or are you simply bored with the same old humdrum menus you've been cooking for years?

The answer to these problems is menu planning. This involves more than just finding two or three dishes that complement each other. It requires organization, but your shopping will be made easier and your cooking more relaxed.

Plan your menus around dishes which can be prepared a day or several days in advance. If you are entertaining, select dishes which can be left to cook unattended or which require little or no last-minute cooking. If you have a small family, plan two or three days ahead so that you can use up leftovers. And don't forget meals based on basics like eggs, cheese and ready-to-eat convenience foods.

This book gives you interchangeable dishes and menus to suit a great variety of occasions — from buffets to suppers on a tray — as well as different budgets and diets. There are exciting meals with a foreign flavour and, a real plus if there are just two of you, how to make multiple and varied meals from one cut of meat. We also give you suggestions for keeping the store cupboard well stocked — most essential for an organized cook.

So turn the page — there are loads of ideas here for interesting and exciting meals.

CONTENTS

First Courses and Light Meals

Avocado Mousse ... 94
Avocado and Seafood Salad ... 95
Bacon and Mushroom Scramble ... 63
Bismarck Hering Salat ... 43
Buckling and Lemon Pâté ... 48
Buttered Noodles or Tagliatelle ... 25
Caviare Forret ... 44
Chilled Seafood Appetizer ... 94
Country Pâté ... 48
Courgettes (Zucchini) à la Grecque ... 94
Creamy Topped Scallops ... 49
Eggs Aurore with Sour Cream ... 21
French Onion Soup ... 84
Fresh Tomato Salad ... 13
Fried Whitebait ... 106
Gaxpacho Andaluz ... 39
Grapefruit and Avocado Vinaigrette ... 27
Greek Island Salad ... 95
Homemade Cornish Pasties ... 64
Homemade Muesli ... 63
Iced Carrot Soup ... 49
Iced Watercress Soup ... 22
Leek and Potato Soup ... 95
Marinated Kippers ... 106
Melanzane Ripiene ... 40
Melon ... 17
Mushrooms à la Grecque ... 14
Oeufs en cocotte ... 33
Pepperpot Beef Soup ... 31
Philly Whizz ... 18
Picnic Pâté ... 91
Quick Liver Pâté ... 8
Quick Pea and Bacon Soup ... 28
Ratatouille ... 35
Smoked Salmon Mousse ... 94
Smoked Salmon and Trout Pâté ... 83
Smoked Trout Mousse ... 49
Taramasalata ... 36
Toasted Oatcakes with Bacon and Apple ... 63
Tortilla ... 64
Tuna Stuffed Lemons ... 95
Turkish Cheese Boreks ... 11
Welsh Rarebit ... 54

Main Dishes

Alpine Eggs ... 80
Anchovy Eggs Mornay ... 25
Baked Fish Provençale ... 22

Beef Carbonnade ... 8
Boeuf en Daube ... 35
Braised Pork with Apples ... 70
Californian Hamburger ... 88
Cannelloni ... 75
Cauliflower Cheese ... 79
Cheese, Egg and Mushroom Tart ... 80
Cheese and Spinach Flan ... 27
Cheese Soufflé ... 17
Chef's Salad ... 72
Chicken in Cider ... 104
Chicken Kiev ... 14
Chicken Risotto ... 116
Chicken Veronique ... 66
Cold Curried Chicken ... 11
Cold Roast Duck with Cherries ... 18
Cottage Pie ... 96
Creamy Veal Pie ... 52
Crisp Pancake Rolls ... 116
Curried Eggs ... 70
Danewiches ... 87
Deep-fried Lamb Croquettes ... 98
Duck ... 75
Duck with Turnips ... 104
Florentine Plaice (Flounder) Fillets ... 66
French Rabbit Stew ... 51
Fried Herrings ... 28
Frikadeller ... 44
Grilled Mackerel with Gooseberry Sauce ... 109
Haddock with Prawn and Mushroom Sauce ... 106
Hazelnut and Tomato Rissoles ... 79
Herby Beef Loaf ... 52
Herrings in Oatmeal ... 109
Instant Chilli con Carne ... 66
Lasagne al Forno ... 33
Meat Loaf ... 64
Minced Beef Curry ... 96
Moussaka ... 116
Nasi Goreng ... 21
Osso Bucco ... 40
Paella ... 39
Picnic Pie ... 91
Piperade Basque ... 76
Poached Trout with Herbs ... 76
Portuguese Fish Steaks ... 84
Ragout of Mutton ... 70
Roast Beef with Roast Potatoes ... 96
Roast Lamb with New Potatoes ... 98
Roast Stuffed Spring Chicken ... 104

Roast Stuffed Turkey with Cranberry Sauce 100
Salmon Loaf 72
Sauerkraut mit Knackwurst 43
Savoury Croquettes 114
Savoury Meat Pie 114
Shish Kebabs 36
Simple Strogonoff 69
Sole with Creamy Sauce and Iced Grapes 109
Somerset Pork 51
Spaghetti alla Carbonara 72
Spiced Chicken 75
Spiced Mutton Pie 114
Steak Tartare 76
Traditional Irish Stew with
  Parsley Dumplings 69
Trout with Almonds 106
Tuna Gratin with Dill 13
Turkey Divan 100
Turkey with Wine Sauce 100
Turkish Lamb Pilaff 98
Veal Cutlets baked with Cream and
  Mushrooms 83
Veal Marengo 69
Vegetable Curry 79
Vol-au-vent Special with Peanuts and
  Raisins 51

Vegetables and Salads
Brussels Sprouts with Chestnuts 103
Buttered Cauliflower 103
Courgettes (Zucchini) with Tomatoes 103
Creamed Potatoes with Spring Onions 102
Guacamole 88
New Potatoes with Mint and Chives 103
Pilau Rice 117
Salade Nicoise 31
Spiced Red Cabbage 103

Desserts
Aeblekage 44
Apple Pan Dowdy 54
Apricot Cheesecake 11
Apricot Cinnamon Crumble 113
Autumn Pudding 28
Baklava 36
Banana and Walnut Cake 91
Banana and Walnut Cream 27
Brigade Pudding 8
Caramelized Peaches and Pears 113

Chocolate Cream Mould 33
Churros 39
Coeurs à la Crème 80
Cream Cup Dessert 111
Crème Brulée 55
Figs with Pernod 83
Fresh Fruit and Cheese 31
Fresh Lemon Jelly 113
Fresh Orange Jelly 22
Fruit Salad Flan 17
Hot Chocolate Fudge Sundae 88
Lemon Soufflé Omelette Flambé 84
Lemon Sponge Pudding 111
Nutty Butterscotch Dessert 13
Orange or Grapefruit Sorbet 18
Pears with Chocolate Sauce 113
Pineapple Waffles 111
Poires au Vin Rouge 35
Profiteroles 55
Queen of Puddings 55
Quick Lemon Crunch 25
Rapsberry Ice Cream 21
Schwarzwalder – Torte 43
Syllabub 14
Treacle Tart 111
Zabaglione 40

Miscellaneous
Cheese Scones (Biscuits) 80
Garlic Cheese Dip 88

Basic Recipes and Methods
Bechamel Sauce 58
Cheese Sauce 117
Cherry Sauce 117
Choux Pastry 56
Flan Case, baking blind 56
French Dressing 58
Frying 57
Giblet Stock 117
Mayonnaise 58
Meringues 57
Pancake Batter 117
Shortcrust Pastry 56
Steaming 56
Stock 57
Suet Crust Pastry 56
Tomato Sauce 57, 117
White Sauce 57

Equivalents for Basic Foods

	British	American	Metric
Breadcrumbs: dry	6 ounces	1 cup	160 grams
fresh	2 ounces	1 cup	60 grams
Butter	$\frac{1}{2}$ ounce	1 tablespoon	15 grams
	4 ounces	$\frac{1}{2}$ cup	125 grams
	1 pound	2 cups	500 grams
Cheese, grated	3 ounces	1 cup	80 grams
Cornflour	$\frac{1}{3}$ ounce	1 tablespoon	10 grams
Plain flour	$1\frac{1}{4}$ ounces	$\frac{1}{4}$ cup	35 grams
	$2\frac{1}{2}$ ounces	$\frac{1}{2}$ cup	70 grams
	5 ounces	1 cup	142 grams
	1 pound	$3\frac{1}{2}$ cups	500 grams
Self-raising flour	1 ounce	$\frac{1}{4}$ cup	30 grams
	2 ounces	$\frac{1}{2}$ cup	60 grams
	4 ounces	1 cup	120 grams
Raisins, seedless	$\frac{1}{3}$ ounce	1 tablespoon	10 grams
	$5\frac{1}{2}$ ounces	1 cup	156 grams
	1 pound	3 cups	500 grams
Rice	8 ounces	1 cup	240 grams
Castor sugar	$\frac{1}{2}$ ounce	1 tablespoon	15 grams
	4 ounces	$\frac{1}{2}$ cup	120 grams
	8 ounces	1 cup	240 grams
Brown sugar	$\frac{1}{3}$ ounce	1 tablespoon	10 grams
	3 ounces	$\frac{1}{2}$ cup	80 grams
	6 ounces	1 cup	160 grams

SUPER MEALS
FOR FRIENDS AND FAMILY
Beef Carbonnade

RICH AND WARMING SUPPER

This menu is ideal to serve on a cold winter's day and should please everyone. The quick pâté can be made just before the meal, if you like, but the flavour will improve if it is made earlier in the day and refrigerated.

The Beef Carbonnade is a simple-to-make basic casserole, given a tasty lift by the addition of beer, but you could always replace the beer with beef stock, or water and a stock cube. It can be made earlier in the day and reheated if need be, or it may be kept in the deep freeze for a later date.

The Brigade Pudding, a mixture of light suet pastry, mincemeat and apples, will steam happily by itself without any attention, apart from checking from time to time to see that the water has not boiled away. Providing that it is not cooking too rapidly it will not matter if you steam it for a bit longer than the suggested time.

For a simple family supper you may like to serve the Carbonnade with a glass of lager or light ale, and omit the pâté. For a more special occasion serve a claret with the meal and offer a selection of cheeses, such as Danish Blue, Cheddar and a herby cream cheese.

Quick Liver Pâté

SERVES 4

6 oz. good quality liver sausage
1 small onion, finely chopped
4 tablespoons single [light] cream
1 small clove garlic, crushed (optional)
1 tablespoon dry sherry or brandy (optional)
salt and freshly milled black pepper
To garnish:
chopped parsley

Remove the skin and fat from the liver sausage and mash with a fork. Add the onion and cream, and the garlic and sherry or brandy if these are being used, to the sausage and mix well. Season to taste. Pile up in a small bowl and sprinkle with chopped parsley. Serve with hot toast and butter.

Beef Carbonnade

SERVES 4

Oven temperature:
Moderate 350°F (Gas Mark 4, 180°C)
Cooking time:
About 2 hours

1½ lb. stewing steak, use chuck or skirt
4 tablespoons lard, dripping, or cooking oil
2 large onions, chopped
4 tablespoons flour
½ pint [1¼ cups] light ale
5 fl. oz. water
¼ teaspoon dried thyme
1 bay leaf
1 teaspoon sugar
salt and pepper

Cut the beef into 1½-inch cubes. Heat the lard, dripping or oil in a saucepan or heatproof casserole and brown the meat quickly in this on all sides. Remove the meat from the pan, then fry the onions until golden. Blend in the flour and cook for 1 minute. Gradually stir in the beer and water, bring to the boil, stirring well, and allow to thicken. Add the meat and remaining ingredients. Cover the pan or casserole, and either simmer gently over a low heat or cook in a moderate oven for about 2 hours until the meat is tender. Adjust the seasoning. Serve with jacket potatoes with plenty of butter and lightly cooked green cabbage.

Brigade Pudding

SERVES 4

Cooking time:
About 2½ hours

2 large cooking apples
10 oz. [1½ cups] mincemeat
2 tablespoons golden [corn] syrup
8 oz. suet crust pastry (see page 54)

Peel the apples, grate them coarsely and add to the mincemeat. Mix well. Grease a 2-3-pint pudding basin and put the syrup in the bottom. Make up the suet crust pastry, following the recipe on page 54. Roll the pastry out thinly and cut out 4 circles, one the size of the bottom of the basin, one the size of the top of the basin, and two in between. Put the smallest circle of pastry into the basin and cover with just under a third of the mincemeat mixture. Top with the next circle of pastry and more mincemeat, and continue in this way ending with the largest circle of pastry. Cover the basin with a double layer of greased greaseproof paper or foil. Either put into a steamer over boiling water or, if you do not have a steamer, stand the basin on a metal pastry cutter in a saucepan of water and simmer gently; the pastry cutter prevents any possibility of the basin cracking. Steam the pudding for about 2½ hours. Turn out of the basin and serve with fresh cream.

above: Brigade Pudding
right: Quick Liver Pâté

BUFFET SUPPER

A buffet supper party is one of the easiest and most relaxed ways to entertain friends. Here, the first course is served hot and the next two cold, so that you spend as much time as possible with your guests.

The Turkish Cheese Boreks may sound rather elaborate, but are, in fact, very easy to make. They can be assembled earlier in the day and kept in the refrigerator until you are ready to bake them.

The lightly curried cold chicken is delicious when served with a green salad and a simple rice salad—made by tossing freshly boiled rice in well seasoned French dressing while it is still warm. When it has cooled, add chopped parsley, walnuts, green pepper, onion, and a few halved and de-seeded grapes.

The Apricot Cheesecake, which is creamy and light in texture, is a good ending to this meal, and a well chilled Pouilly Fumé or similar dry white wine would go well with it.

opposite: Turkish Cheese Boreks
Cold Curried Chicken
Apricot Cheesecake

Turkish Cheese Boreks

SERVES 8

Oven temperature:
Very hot 450°F (Gas Mark 8, 230°C)
Cooking time:
About 12 minutes

1 × 13 oz. packet puff pastry, defrosted
8 oz. Emmenthal cheese, very thinly sliced
1 egg, beaten

For the topping:
6 oz. [¾ cup] cream cheese
little milk
1½ tablespoons chopped chives
1 tablespoon chopped parsley
1 clove garlic, crushed
salt and pepper

Roll the puff pastry out thinly, and cut out 32 x 3½-inch circles. Put 8 of these on to a damp baking sheet, and cover with a slice of cheese the same size as the pastry circle. Add a second pastry circle, dampened with water. Continue until, in each borek, you have 4 layers of pastry and 3 of cheese. Brush the top of each with beaten egg, and bake for about 12 minutes or until the pastry is well risen and golden brown.
Serve at once, topped with the cold cream cheese mixture.
To make the topping, soften the cheese with a little milk, blend in the herbs, garlic and seasoning, and chill.

Cold Curried Chicken

SERVES 8

Cooking time:
1½ hours

5-6 lb. chicken
1 onion
¼ teaspoon ground mace
6 peppercorns
sprig of thyme
peeled zest 1 lemon
few sprigs parsley
1 teaspoon salt
1¾ pints [4½ cups] water
For the sauce:
4 tablespoons butter
5 tablespoons flour
1 tablespoon mild curry powder
1¼ pints [3 cups] chicken stock from cooking the chicken
2 tablespoons red currant jelly
5 fl. oz. sour cream or 5 fl. oz. double cream [heavy] and 1 tablespoon lemon juice
salt and pepper
To garnish:
paprika and green grapes

Put the chicken into a saucepan with the onion, mace, peppercorns, thyme, lemon zest, parsley, salt and water.
Cover and bring to the boil. Simmer gently for 1½ hours until tender.
Allow the chicken to cool in the stock, then remove from the pan. Cut the meat off the chicken bones and cut into medium-sized pieces. Remove any excess fat from the chicken stock. Melt the butter for the sauce in a pan and stir in the flour and curry powder. Cook for about 2 minutes without browning. Gradually stir in the chicken stock and bring to the boil, stirring all the time. Allow to simmer for about 5 minutes. Remove from the heat and stir in the red currant jelly. Cover the sauce with a circle of damp greaseproof paper and allow to cool. When the sauce is cold, remove the greaseproof paper, add the cream and season to taste. Stir in the chicken and spoon on to a serving plate. Sprinkle with paprika and garnish with small bunches of green grapes.
Serve with rice and green salads.

Apricot Cheesecake

SERVES 8

1 packet orange jelly [jello, made with ½ the water]
1 lb. 12 oz. canned apricot halves
1 lb. cottage cheese, sieved
2 tablespoons sugar
5 fl. oz. double [heavy] cream, whipped
10 ginger biscuits [snaps]
2 tablespoons soft brown sugar
4 tablespoons melted butter

Put the jelly into a saucepan with 3 tablespoons of apricot juice from the can. Put over a very gentle heat and stir from time to time until the jelly has dissolved. It must not be allowed to boil.
Reserve 6 apricot halves for decoration. Drain and chop (or sieve) the rest, and mix with the cottage cheese and sugar. Stir in the cooled jelly and carefully fold in the whipped cream. Turn the mixture into a lightly oiled 8-inch round cake tin. Chill.
Put half the biscuits into a clean cloth, or between two sheets of waxed paper, and crush with a rolling pin. Repeat with the remaining biscuits and mix them all with the sugar and butter. When the cheesecake has set sufficiently sprinkle the biscuit mixture over the top and press it down lightly. Chill until set. Turn the cheesecake out by inverting the tin over a serving plate. Decorate with apricot halves.
Note: The Cheesecake may be glazed with apricot jam, melted with water.

QUICK SUPPER

left: Fresh Tomato Salad
Tuna Gratin with Dill
above: Nutty Butterscotch Dessert

Suppers which are both quick to prepare and cook, and are not exorbitantly expensive, are often very difficult to plan. The entire menu given here can be done in just over 30 minutes, so it is an excellent supper to serve if you arrive home late after having been out all day, or have unexpected guests. It is not entirely a store-cupboard meal, but you are quite likely to have the other ingredients in the house anyway.

A Fresh Tomato Salad is always popular and can be varied in any way you like, according to the ingredients you have available, and the time of year. This salad is also excellent served as part of a mixed hors d'oeuvre, with cold meat, or with the soufflé.

The Tuna Gratin with Dill is a delicious, but simple, recipe which could be made equally as well with salmon, if preferred. The basic sauce mixture can also be made into a pie using either short or puff pastry, or into individual fish patties with puff pastry.

The Nutty Butterscotch Dessert is made from a packet of instant dessert mix with cream and nuts folded into it. To save time, you might omit the pudding and serve fruit instead. If you would like to serve a wine with the meal a medium dry white, such as a Graves, would go well with it.

Fresh Tomato Salad

SERVES 4

1 lb. tomatoes
3 tablespoons French dressing (see page 56)
½ teaspoon dried or 2 teaspoons fresh chopped basil
½ small onion, very finely chopped

Peel the tomatoes. This is not essential but, especially if the skins are rather thick, does improve the salad. A quick way of peeling the tomatoes is to cover them with boiling water, for about a minute. The skins should then slip off easily. Slice and put into a serving dish.
Mix the basil with the French dressing and pour over the tomatoes. Sprinkle with the finely chopped onion.

Variations:
The above is only a very basic tomato salad and a great many additions and variations can be made:

§Add thin slices or small pieces of Mozzarella cheese, or crumble a little Danish Blue cheese over the top.
§Omit the basil, and use 2 teaspoons of chopped parsley and 2 teaspoons of chopped chives.
§Add a crushed clove of garlic to the French Dressing.
§Add 2 finely chopped gherkins to the French Dressing.
§Use only 8 ounces of tomatoes, and add ¼ thinly sliced cucumber or 2 pickled cucumbers, sliced.

Tuna Gratin with Dill

SERVES 4

Cooking time:
About 15 minutes

3 tablespoons butter or margarine
1 onion, finely chopped
4 tablespoons flour
¾ pint [2 cups] milk
¼ teaspoon dried dill
7 oz. canned tuna

salt and freshly milled black pepper
1 oz. [⅓ cup] fresh breadcrumbs
1½ oz. [⅓ cup] grated Cheddar cheese

Melt the butter or margarine in a pan and fry the onion gently for about 5 minutes until transparent. Blend in the flour and cook for 1 minute. Gradually stir in the milk and bring to the boil, stirring all the time. Add the dill and flaked tuna together with the oil from the can. Season to taste with salt and pepper. Turn into an ovenproof dish.
Mix the breadcrumbs with the cheese and sprinkle over the top of the fish mixture. Put under the grill [broiler] and grill for about 5 minutes or until golden brown.
Serve with peas and canned or fresh new potatoes.

Variation:
Use 1 can concentrated mushroom soup instead of the sauce.

Nutty Butterscotch Dessert

SERVES 4

1 pint packet instant Butterscotch dessert mix
generous ¾ pint [2 cups] milk
2 oz. [½ cup] walnuts, almonds or brazil nuts, chopped
5 fl. oz. double [heavy] cream, whipped

Make up the dessert following the instructions on the packet, but using only ¾ pint [2 cups] milk. Allow to thicken slightly, then fold in most of the nuts and the cream. Turn into 4 individual dishes.
When set, top with the remaining cream and chopped nuts.

Variations:
§Use a chocolate dessert mix instead of the Butterscotch.
§Make up the mix with a full pint of milk. When it has set spread the whipped cream on top, and sprinkle the chopped nuts in a thick layer to complete.

ELEGANT SUPPER

This menu would be ideal for a rather special occasion. If you have invited friends for supper, perhaps on their birthday or wedding anniversary, you will want to create an elegant impression.
If a celebration is involved you may like to serve champagne with the meal, but otherwise a chilled Liebfraumilch or similar dry white wine would be very suitable.

The Chicken Kiev is not, however, an expensive dish and could also be served for a family supper with the mushrooms as a first course, and fruit and cheese as dessert rather than the Syllabub.

The only slightly tricky part of this meal is the preparation of the Chicken Kiev. It is important that the chicken is boned carefully so that the flesh is not split, and that after the butter has been put on the breast the meat is rolled up well so that the butter is completely sealed in. If this is not done properly all the butter will seep out during cooking and you will not have the delicious pool of melted butter inside the chicken when you open it.
If, however, you see that butter is oozing out of the chicken during the frying, you can quickly make up some more herb butter to serve with the chicken.

Mushrooms à la Grecque

SERVES 4

Cooking time:
5 minutes

5 fl. oz. water
juice of ½ lemon
2 tablespoons olive oil
sprig of thyme or good pinch dried thyme
1 bay leaf
1-2 cloves garlic, crushed
1 tablespoon concentrated tomato purée
salt and freshly milled black pepper
8 oz. small button mushrooms

Put all the ingredients except the mushrooms into a saucepan, and bring to the boil. Add the washed, but not peeled, mushrooms and simmer gently for about 5 minutes.
Remove from the heat and allow to cool. Refrigerate for about 4 hours, until well chilled.

Chicken Kiev

SERVES 4

Cooking time:
About 12 minutes

4 breast of chicken pieces
4 oz. [½ cup] butter
1 tablespoon chopped parsley
1 tablespoon chopped chives
salt and pepper
1 egg beaten with 1 tablespoon water
dried breadcrumbs
deep fat or oil for frying

Remove the breast bone from each chicken joint, taking great care not to break the flesh of the bird. Skin the chicken breast and cut off the first two bones of the wings. Scrape back the meat from the remaining bone.
Put each chicken breast between two sheets of wet greaseproof paper and pound until thin, taking care not to split the meat.
Cream the butter until soft, then beat in the parsley and chives. Divide the butter into four and place one on each chicken breast. Season with salt and pepper.
Roll the meat up envelope fashion, so that the wing bone protrudes, making sure that the butter is well sealed. Toss in seasoned flour, dip in the beaten egg and roll in breadcrumbs. If you like you can coat the chicken twice in egg and crumbs so that the butter is really well sealed in. Chill for at least 1 hour.
Deep fry the chicken in hot fat or oil for about 12 minutes.
Serve with courgettes [zucchini] or broccoli, and Duchesse potatoes.

Note: Make Duchesse potatoes by adding 2 egg yolks to every pound of mashed and sieved potato, with salt and pepper to taste. Put the mixture into a piping bag, and pipe rosettes of potato on to a greased baking sheet. Bake these in a fairly hot oven, for about 15 minutes.

Syllabub

SERVES 4

grated zest and juice 1 large lemon
4 tablespoons sweet sherry
2 tablespoons brandy
4 tablespoons castor [fine] sugar
½ pint double cream [1¼ cups heavy cream]

Put the grated lemon zest and juice into a bowl with the sherry, brandy and sugar. Stir until sugar has dissolved.
Add the cream and whisk until the mixture forms soft peaks. Spoon into four glasses and chill.

opposite: top left: Syllabub
top right: Mushrooms à la Grecque
right: Chicken Kiev

LIGHT SUPPER

right: *Fruit Salad Flan*
below: *ingredients for*
Cheese Soufflé

A light supper makes a refreshing change after a heavy lunch, or if you are eating late at night. On such occasions a soufflé is a very light, yet tasty dish to serve, and contrary to popular opinion, is not difficult to make.

The important points to remember are to beat the egg whites stiffly, (but not so stiffly that they are difficult to fold in), and to fold them carefully and evenly into the egg yolk mixture. Since a soufflé does not take long to prepare, you can put it into the oven about 10 minutes before serving the melon, and it will be ready at just the right time.

Although given here as a main course it can be served as a first course, which would serve 6-8. If preferred, the mixture could then be cooked in individual dishes—at the same temperature, but for 10-15 minutes, instead of 30 minutes.

The Fruit Salad Flan can be made with any fruit, or mixture of fruits, that you choose. The base of the flan is covered with a layer of pastry cream (although whipped double [heavy] cream could be used instead) which is then topped with the fruit, and an arrowroot glaze is spooned over the top of the mixture.

If you should wish to serve a wine with this meal a well-chilled light Anjou Rosé would be a good accompaniment to the Cheese Soufflé.

Melon

Melon can be served in a variety of ways as an hors d'oeuvre. Melons should not be stored in the refrigerator as this destroys their flavour, but they should be chilled for an hour before serving. Some of the most usual melons are green and yellow Honeydew melons, Charentais, Cantaloupe and Ogen melons.

§Melon with Parma ham
Put peeled slices of melon on a plate with thin slices of Parma ham. Garnish with lemon wedges. Coppe, Bündnerfleisch or good York ham could be substituted for the Parma ham.

§Melon with fresh strawberries
Scoop the melon into balls, using a Parisienne cutter and put into a glass with an equal quantity of fresh strawberries. Spoon over any melon juice.

§Melon with port
Halve a small Charentias or Ogen melon (sufficient for 2 people). Remove the seeds from the melon and spoon some port into the hole that is left.

Cheese Soufflé

SERVES 4

Oven temperature:
Fairly hot 375°F (Gas Mark 5, 190°C)
Cooking time:
About 30 minutes

2 tablespoons butter or margarine
4 tablespoons flour
generous 5 fl. oz. milk
3 oz. [¾ cup] strong Cheddar cheese, grated
4 eggs, separated
salt and freshly milled black pepper
½ teaspoon made mustard

Heat the butter or margarine in a large saucepan. Add the flour and cook for about 1 minute. Gradually blend in the milk, bring to the boil and stir until thickened. Remove from the heat and stir in the cheese. Beat the egg yolks in one at a time and season with salt, pepper and mustard. Stiffly whisk the egg whites and fold into the cheese mixture. Turn into a 2½-pint soufflé dish and bake in a fairly hot oven for about 30 minutes or until well risen and golden brown.
Serve with a Fresh Tomato Salad.

§Smoked haddock soufflé
Use 4 ounces [½ cup] flaked cooked haddock in place of the cheese.

§ Ham soufflé
Use 4 ounces [½ cup] finely chopped ham in place of the cheese.

Fruit Salad Flan

SERVES 4-6

Oven temperature:
Fairly hot 400°F (Gas Mark 6, 200°C)
Cooking time:
20 minutes

6 oz. short crust pastry
1 egg
2 tablespoons flour
2 tablespoons sugar
5 fl. oz. milk
1 tablespoon butter or margarine
few drops vanilla essence
15 oz. canned fruit or fresh fruit in season
For the glaze:
1½ teaspoons arrowroot
5 fl. oz. fruit juice from the can or sugar syrup made from 5 fl. oz. water and 3 tablespoons sugar

Make up the pastry, line a 7-inch flan ring and bake blind (see page 54). Blend the egg and beat in the flour and sugar. Bring the milk to the boil and pour over the egg mixture, stirring. Return to the pan and bring to the boil, stirring all the time until thick. Cook for 1-2 minutes. Remove from the heat and stir in the butter or margarine and vanilla essence. Cover with a circle of damp greaseproof or waxed paper and leave to cool.

When the pastry cream and flan case are cold, spread the pastry cream over the base of the flan. Drain the canned fruit well, or core or stone the fresh fruit, and slice thinly. (It is not necessary to peel fruit such as apples, as the skin gives colour). If the fruit discolours easily, such as apples and bananas, dip the slices in lemon juice to preserve the colour. Arrange the fruit attractively over the top of the pastry cream.
Blend the arrowroot with 1 tablespoon of the fruit syrup and bring the remainder of the syrup to the boil. Pour over the arrowroot, stirring. Return to the heat and bring to the boil again, stirring all the time until clear. Allow to cool a little, then spoon over the fruit.
Serve with cream.

COOL SUMMER SUPPER

When the weather is hot, one wants to spend as little time as possible in the kitchen. All the recipes given here are designed to comply with this requirement. For instance, if made in a blender, the Philly Whizz literally takes only a minute to make and not much longer if it is done by hand.

In hot weather it is also a good idea to do as much cooking as possible in the oven, rather than on the top of the stove, as this keeps the kitchen cooler. So, for a main course, we suggest Cold Duck with Cherries.

The sauce for the duck has a pleasant 'bite' to it which contrasts well with the rather rich meat. Chicken would also go well with the sauce and may be used if preferred.

The Grapefruit or Orange Sorbet has for its base a can of concentrated frozen fruit juice. This gives the sorbet an excellent, full flavour, which is no trouble at all to make.

If you are planning to entertain this supper is an ideal choice, as there is no last minute cooking to be done. A chilled Moselle or other light white wine would be an appropriate choice to serve with it.

Philly Whizz

SERVES 4

10 fl. oz. [1¼ cups] canned consommé
3 oz. cream cheese
1 tablespoon chopped chives

Blend the consommé gradually into the cheese, using a spoon and then a whisk, until you have a smooth, creamy mixture. Alternatively, put into a blender and switch on until well mixed. Place in 4 individual dishes and sprinkle with chopped chives. *Chill* for about 4 hours or until set.

Cold Roast Duck with Cherries

SERVES 4-6

Oven temperature:
Fairly hot 375°F (Gas Mark 5, 190°C)
Moderate 350°F (Gas Mark 4, 180°C)
Cooking time:
2 hours

1 × 5 lb. duck
salt and pepper
1 small onion, peeled
15 oz. canned black cherries
4 tablespoons mayonnaise
juice of 1 large orange
3 tablespoons French dressing
2 teaspoons chopped parsley

Put the duck into a roasting tin and prick the skin all over with a fork. Season with salt and pepper. Place the onion inside the bird. Roast the duck in a fairly hot oven for 20 minutes, then lower the heat to moderate and continue cooking for a further 1 hour 40 minutes. Strain the syrup from the, cherries and spoon this syrup over the duck half way through cooking. Baste with the syrup from time to time. *Allow* the duck to cool, then carve neatly and arrange on a serving plate. Cover and keep in a cool place until ready to serve. Stone the cherries. Blend together the mayonnaise, orange juice, French dressing and parsley. Stir in most of the cherries and chill.

Spoon the sauce over the duck just before serving and top with the remaining cherries.
Serve with sliced cooked new potatoes and cold cooked peas.

Orange or Grapefruit Sorbet

SERVES 4

10 oz. canned mandarin oranges or
14 oz. canned grapefruit segments
6 fl. oz. [¾ cup] canned frozen orange or grapefruit juice concentrate, defrosted
1 egg white

Drain the juice from the fruit and make up to ½ pint [1¼ cups] with water, if necessary. Add the orange or grapefruit juice to the fruit syrup and mix well. Pour into a 1-pint plastic container with a lid.
Put this into the refrigerator at the coldest setting, or into the freezer, and freeze for about 1 hour or until almost firm.
Turn into a bowl and mash with a fork so that no large lumps remain. Stiffly whisk the egg white and fold into the mixture. Return to the plastic container, cover and freeze. To serve the sorbet, scoop it out from the container, using a tablespoon or ice cream scoop, on to a serving dish. Decorate with the segments of mandarin orange or grapefruit.

Note: If you wish to make this sorbet and keep it for some time in the freezer, instead of using the syrup from the can of fruit, make up a syrup using 10 fl. oz. water and 6 tablespoons sugar. Put over a low heat until the sugar has dissolved. Soften ¼ ounce [1 tablespoon] gelatine in 2 tablespoons water, add to the hot syrup and dissolve, then continue as above.
The addition of the gelatine prevents the formation of large ice splinters, which occur after prolonged freezing.

opposite: Philly Whizz
Cold Roast Duck with Cherries
Cold Peas and Potatoes
Orange Sorbet

T.V. SUPPER

A good programme on television often involves the planning of a meal which the family can eat from trays. The dishes here are entirely suitable for such a meal, being easy both to eat and to serve. If only a two course meal is wanted, omit the Eggs Aurore: for a simpler three course meal, serve fresh fruit instead of the ice cream.

The Eggs Aurore with Sour Cream is a quick first course which can be put on the trays as soon as it is made.

Nasi Goreng is a classic Indonesian dish which, like many Indonesian specialities, is very popular in Holland. Provided that it is put on to a hot plate and covered with foil or a second hot plate it will remain piping hot until the first course has been eaten.

There are few things more delicious than a home made ice-cream. This particular recipe is not difficult and does not need to be taken from the freezer and beaten during the freezing process. Once it is made, you can forget all about it. If the ice cream is removed from the freezer or a cold ice box and placed in glasses just before serving the meal, it should be the right temperature when the first two courses have been eaten.

Eggs Aurore with Sour Cream

SERVES 4

Cooking time:
10 minutes

4 eggs
5 fl. oz. sour cream, or 5 fl. oz. double [heavy] cream mixed with 1 tablespoon lemon juice
2 tablespoons mayonnaise
2 tablespoons tomato ketchup
1 teaspoon made mustard
2 tablespoons chopped olives
salt and pepper
To garnish:
paprika
halved stoned olives

Hard boil the eggs for 10 minutes. Put into cold water, shell and cut in half lengthways. Place two halved eggs on each of four individual serving plates, with the cut side downwards. *Blend* together the sour cream, mayonnaise, tomato ketchup, mustard and chopped olives. Season to taste and spoon over the eggs. Sprinkle with paprika and garnish with halved stoned olives.
Serve with brown bread and butter.

Nasi Goreng

SERVES 4

Cooking time:
30 minutes

12 oz. [2 cups] long grain rice
1 lb. frozen mixed vegetables
1¼ lb. shoulder of pork
3 large onions
4 oz. [½ cup] butter or margarine
3 tablespoons soy sauce
1½ teaspoons mild curry powder
salt and pepper

Cook the rice in boiling salted water for 12 minutes. Drain, and rinse under cold water to remove all the surplus starch. Drain again. Cook the mixed vegetables in boiling salted water following the instructions on the packet. Drain well. Cut the pork into cubes and slice the onions in rings.

Heat half the butter in a large pan and fry the onions and pork for about 20 minutes over a medium heat. Turn from time to time. Add the remaining butter, the rice, mixed vegetables, soy sauce, curry powder and seasoning. Mix well and heat until piping hot.
Serve with a green salad, peanuts and shrimp crisps.

Raspberry Ice Cream

SERVES 4

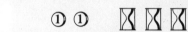

1 lb. fresh or frozen raspberries
sieved icing [confectioners'] sugar
2 eggs, separated
5 fl. oz. double [heavy] cream, whipped

Sieve the raspberries or put into a blender. Sweeten to taste with icing sugar. Beat egg yolks and 4 tablespoons of icing sugar until thick and creamy. Whisk the egg whites until stiff, then whisk in 4 tablespoons icing sugar. Gradually whisk in the egg yolk mixture. Finally fold in the raspberry pureé and cream. Turn into a freezing tray and freeze until firm.
Serve scoops of the ice cream in glasses with biscuits [plain cookies].

opposite: top: Eggs Aurore with Sour Cream
left: Nasi Goreng

SLIMMERS' SUPPER

People often feel that a slimmers' meal must of necessity be dull, boring and rather tasteless.
This menu should, however, dispel these illusions forever; while being low in calories, the dishes look attractive and taste just as good.

The Iced Watercress Soup should be made earlier in the day and refrigerated. If a soup tureen takes up too much room in your refrigerator, you may find it more practical to chill the soup in a jug and turn it into the tureen just before serving. To chill the tureen, just put a few ice cubes into the bottom and leave it for about 10 minutes. Empty out the tureen and wipe dry.

If it is more convenient the foil parcels of fish, which make a complete course in themselves, can be made a few hours earlier and kept in the refrigerator before baking. It is important with this dish to time the cooking carefully, as fish spoils if it is overcooked.

For a simple two-course family supper, omit the soup. If you are entertaining and wish to serve a wine with the meal, a dry white wine, such as a German hock would not only go well with the fish, but is also the lowest in calories.

Iced Watercress Soup

SERVES 4

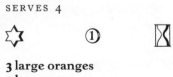

Cooking time:
30 minutes

2 large bunches watercress
2 tablespoons butter
2 spring onions [scallions], chopped
½ chicken stock cube
1 pint [2½ cups] water
5 fl. oz. natural yogurt
2 egg yolks
salt and pepper

Wash and chop the watercress, reserving a few sprigs for garnish.
Melt the butter in a large pan and cook the spring onions gently, until soft.
Add the watercress, stock cube and water, and bring to the boil. Cover and simmer for 20 minutes.
Either rub now, through a sieve, or put the mixture into a blender; return it then to rinsed pan. Beat together the yogurt and egg yolks, and gradually add to the soup. Reheat gently without boiling, and adjust the seasoning. Turn into a soup tureen and chill for about 3 hours.
Serve garnished with a few ice cubes and the reserved sprigs of watercress.

Baked Fish Provençale

SERVES 4

Oven temperature:
Fairly hot 400 °F (Gas Mark 6, 200°C)
Cooking time:
40 minutes

4 cod steaks or 4 fillets of haddock
4 tomatoes
4 oz. mushrooms
1 green pepper
1 tablespoon chopped parsley
salt and pepper

Put each steak or fillet of fish on to a square of foil. Peel and slice the tomatoes, and slice the mushrooms. Blanch the pepper in boiling water for 2 minutes, then slice, discarding the core and seeds. Put a few tomatoes, mushroom and pepper slices on each piece of the fish.
Sprinkle over a little chopped parsley and season well with salt and pepper. Put into a fairly hot oven and bake for about 40 minutes, or until the vegetables are tender and the fish flakes easily.

Fresh Orange Jelly

SERVES 4

3 large oranges
1 lemon
water
½ oz. or 2 tablespoons powdered gelatine
artificial liquid sweetener

Peel the oranges thinly, removing only the orange zest and leaving the white pith. Do the same with the lemon. Put the zest into a saucepan with ½ pint [1¼ cups] water. Simmer for about 10 minutes.
Soften the gelatine in 4 tablespoons of cold water for about 5 minutes. Remove the pan containing the orange and lemon zest from the heat, add the softened gelatine, and stir until dissolved. Strain into a measuring jug.
Squeeze the juice from the oranges and lemons, strain and add to the gelatine mixture. The fruit juice and gelatine mixture should be 1 pint [2½ cups], but if necessary make up with cold water. Sweeten to taste with artificial liquid sweetener. Turn into a bowl or mould and leave to set.

opposite: Iced Watercress Soup
Baked Fish Provençale

PLANNED AROUND EGGS

right: Quick Lemon Crunch
below: Anchovy Eggs Mornay

Eggs are about the most versatile food there is. Apart from being fried, scrambled, poached and boiled, they are used in almost every dish imaginable, both sweet and savoury, as well as being an essential ingredient in cakes.

The Anchovy Eggs Mornay given here are hard-boiled eggs stuffed with anchovies and served with a cheese sauce poured over the top. It is a dish which can either be made and cooked straight away or which can be completely prepared (apart from the final baking) and kept in the refrigerator until required. If doing the latter, however, increase the baking time by about 10 minutes.

The Quick Lemon Crunch has a filling made with canned condensed milk, lemon zest and juice, and cream. The acid of the lemon juice has the effect of setting the condensed milk so that a thick creamy filling results. The crunch is crushed digestive biscuits [graham crackers], butter and sugar.

For a family supper the noodles may be omitted, or the dessert left out and fresh fruit served instead. Apples would be particularly good after the eggs.

To make it into a rather more elaborate meal, hand round herb or garlic bread with the noodles and serve a full-bodied red Burgundy wine.

Buttered Noodles or Tagliatelle

SERVES 4

☆ ① ⋈

Cooking time:
About 12 minutes

10 oz. noodles or tagliatelle
salt
4 tablespoons unsalted butter
freshly milled black pepper

Cook the noodles in a large pan of boiling salted water for about 12 minutes or until the pasta is just tender. Be careful not to overcook them. Drain and rinse well with boiling water, to remove any excess starch, then drain again.
Melt the butter in the saucepan, then add the noodles, tossing them in the butter. Season with plenty of pepper, and serve piping hot.

Variations:
A few easy suggestions.
§Sprinkle the butter tossed noodles generously with grated Parmesan cheese.
§Toss in 2 tablespoons butter and serve with a tomato sauce.
§Add 2 tablespoons chopped mixed fresh herbs (parsley, chives, tarragon, basil) and a crushed clove of garlic.

Anchovy Eggs Mornay

SERVES 4

☆ ⋈

Oven temperature:
Fairly hot 400°F (Gas Mark 6, 200°C)
Cooking time:
About 25 minutes

6 eggs
4 tablespoons single [light] cream
1¾ oz. canned anchovies
freshly milled black pepper
2 tablespoons butter
4 tablespoons flour
½ pint [1¼ cups] milk
6 oz. [1½ cups] grated Cheddar cheese
salt
made mustard

Hard boil the eggs for 10 minutes. Cool quickly and shell. Cut each egg in half lengthways and remove the yolks. Mash the yolks with the cream. Drain the anchovies and chop very finely. Add to the egg yolks, mix well, and season with pepper.
Spoon the yolk mixture back into the white cases and place the eggs, cut side downwards in a lightly greased ovenproof serving dish. Make up a white sauce with the butter, flour and milk. Add most of the cheese to the sauce and season to taste with salt, pepper and mustard. Pour this over the eggs, and sprinkle with the remaining cheese. Cook for about 15 minutes in a fairly hot oven until the cheese is golden brown. Do not overcook as the eggs will become tough.
Serve with spinach and new potatoes.

Variations:
§Add about 2 tablespoons finely chopped watercress or chives to the egg yolks. Season well with salt and pepper.
§Add 2 oz. [¼ cup] minced ham to the egg yolks. Season with salt, pepper and mustard.

Quick Lemon Crunch

SERVES 4

☆ ① ① ⋈

4 oz. digestive biscuits [graham crackers]
4 tablespoons melted butter
1 tablespoon soft brown sugar
10 fl. oz. canned condensed milk
grated zest and juice of 2 large lemons
5 fl. oz. single [light] cream
To decorate:
crystallized lemon slices

Put the biscuits between two pieces of waxed paper and crush with a rolling pin. Mix with the butter and sugar. Divide half the crumb mixture among four dishes. Chill.
Mix together the condensed milk, lemon zest and juice and cream. Divide between the four dishes or glasses and leave for about 10 minutes until set. Top with the remaining crumb mixture and chill for about 2 hours before serving.
Decorate with the slices of crystallized lemon.

left: Cheese and Spinach Flan
below: Grapefruit and Avocado
Vinaigrette

PLANNED AROUND CHEESE

This menu could make a very good family supper: if only two courses are wanted, the first is the most sensible to omit. It would also be an excellent meal to serve to vegetarians. If you are entertaining, try a strong red wine—a Château neuf du Pape, for example.

Grapefruit and avocado, both very popular first courses, are combined here in a rather unusual hors d'oeuvre. They would also go very well as part of a mixed hors d'oeuvre, in which case the quantities should be halved.

The Cheese and Spinach Flan makes good use of cooked cheese without producing an over-rich dish (some people find cooked cheese rather indigestible). The flan can also be used as a first course, and would then serve 6 people.

The Banana and Walnut Cream should not be made more than about 3 hours before serving as otherwise, despite the addition of lemon juice, it will begin to turn brown. You might wish to omit the walnuts for young children, although it is generally a very popular dessert.

Grapefruit and Avocado Vinaigrette

SERVES 4

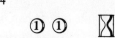

1 large grapefruit
1 large avocado pear
4 tablespoons French dressing
  (see page 56)

Holding the grapefruit over a basin, peel off all the skin and pith, using a very sharp knife. Still holding the grapefruit over the basin, cut out the segments of fruit between the skin and discard any pips. Peel the avocado pear, cut in half and remove the stone. Slice the flesh thinly.
Arrange the grapefruit segments and avocado slices in four individual dishes or glasses. Mix the French dressing with any grapefruit juice in the basin and spoon over the fruit immediately.

Cheese and Spinach Flan

SERVES 4

Oven temperature:
Fairly hot 400°F (Gas Mark 6, 200°C)
            375°F (Gas Mark 5, 190°C)
Cooking time:
About 55 minutes

6 oz. short crust pastry (see page 54)
2 tablespoons butter
1 medium-sized onion, finely
  chopped
1 large egg
5 fl. oz. milk
8 oz. packet frozen chopped
  spinach, defrosted and well
  drained
salt and pepper
¼ teaspoon grated nutmeg
6 oz. cheese (Cheddar, Edam,
  Gruyère or Tilsiter), thinly
  sliced

Make up the pastry, roll out and line an 8-inch flan ring or sandwich tin and bake blind . Lower the oven temperature to 375°F.

Melt the butter in a small pan and fry the onion gently for about 5 minutes. Beat the egg, then beat in the milk, onion and spinach. Season with salt, pepper and nutmeg. Lay half the slices of cheese in the bottom of the flan. Spoon over the spinach mixture and top with the remaining sliced cheese.
Bake at 375°F for about 30 minutes or until the egg is set and the cheese golden brown.
Serve with sauté potatoes sprinkled with chopped chives.

Banana and Walnut Cream

SERVES 4

4 large ripe bananas
juice ½ lemon
4 oz. [½ cup] sugar
2 oz. [½ cup] walnuts, chopped
5 fl. oz. yogurt
5 fl. oz. double [heavy] cream,
  whipped
To decorate:
1 banana
1 tablespoon lemon juice

Mash the peeled bananas with a fork. Blend in the lemon juice, sugar, walnuts and yogurt. Fold in the whipped cream and turn into a serving dish. Chill for about 1 hour.
Thinly slice the banana for decoration, and sprinkle with lemon juice. Arrange it attractively over the top of the banana and cream mixture.

Variations:
§Omit the cream, and double the quantity of yogurt.

§Substitute chopped hazelnuts for the walnuts.

The herring has been described as 'The King of Fish' and rightly too. It has an excellent flavour and is extremely nourishing, but (possibly because it is cheap and plentiful) it it is often neglected. It can be cooked in many ways, but one of the simplest and most delicious is in the traditional Scottish manner, tossed in oatmeal and then fried. Served with Yogurt and Cucumber Sauce it makes an easily prepared, but rather luxurious dish.

The Quick Pea and Bacon Soup makes use of a can of condensed pea soup, and shows how easily a convenience food can be made into something just a little bit special.

Traditional British summer pudding, made with red currants, black currants and raspberries is given a change here and made with the popular autumn combination of blackberries and apples. This is an excellent pudding to make after a day's blackberrying, but frozen blackberries could also be used, so it is a good all-the-year-round dessert as well.

For a family supper, omit the soup, or if you are entertaining you might serve a selection of cheese, such as Brie, fresh cream cheese and Emmenthal, after the Pudding. A chilled Moselle or other light white wine would go very well with this meal.

Quick Pea and Bacon Soup

SERVES 4

Cooking time:
10 minutes

10 fl. oz. canned condensed pea soup
2 tablespoons lard
3 slices streaky bacon
2 slices white bread
4 tablespoons single [light] cream

Empty the contents of the can of soup into a saucepan and make up as directed. Put over a gentle heat.
Heat the lard in a frying pan and fry the bacon until crisp. Remove it from the pan and break into small pieces. Dice the bread into ½-inch pieces and fry in the bacon fat, adding more lard to the pan if necessary.
When the soup is piping hot, stir in the cream, turn into a soup tureen or individual bowls, and sprinkle with the crisp bacon.
Serve the fried croûtons separately.

Fried Herrings

SERVES 4

Cooking time:
About 10 minutes

½ cucumber
salt
5 fl. oz. natural yogurt
1 tablespoon chopped parsley
freshly milled black pepper
4 herrings
about 2 tablespoons medium
   oatmeal
4 tablespoons butter or margarine
1 tablespoon oil

First prepare the sauce. Peel the cucumber and dice it into ¼-inch pieces. Put it into a sieve over a bowl or basin and sprinkle with salt. Leave for about 30 minutes for the excess water in the cucumber to drain off. Mix the cucumber with the yogurt and parsley, and season to taste with pepper.
Remove the heads from the herrings, if you wish, and scale and clean them (or ask the fishmonger to do this for you). Mix ½ teaspoon salt with the oatmeal and roll the herrings in this. Heat the butter or margarine in a frying pan with the oil, and fry the herrings for 4-5 minutes on each side.
Remove from the pan and serve hot with the cold cucumber sauce, and new potatoes and beans.

Autumn Pudding

SERVES 4-6

Cooking time:
About 10 minutes

1 large cooking apple
1 lb. fresh blackberries*
5 fl. oz. water
4 oz. [½ cup] sugar
about 8 thin slices white bread

*Or use 1½ lb. frozen blackberries, defrosted, but in this case do not add water. The blackberries can be cooked in the juice which forms when they defrost.

Peel and core the apple and slice it thinly. Put into a saucepan with the blackberries and water, and simmer until tender. Remove from the heat, stir in the sugar, and allow to cool.
Remove the crusts from the bread. Trim a circle of bread to fit the bottom of a 2-pint pudding basin. Line the sides of the basin with fingers of bread, shaped wider at one end than the other, making sure they fit well together. Add a little fruit and juice, and then cover with a layer of bread. Continue until the basin is full, finishing with a layer of bread: about 3 layers in all. Cover with a plate which fits the top of the basin, and place a heavy weight on top of that. Leave in a refrigerator, or a cool place, for about 8 hours.
Turn out and serve with fresh cream.

PLANNED AROUND FISH

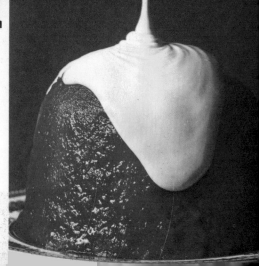

above: Fried Herrings
right: Autumn Pudding

PLANNED AROUND A HEARTY SOUP

During the winter, a good, warming soup can form the basis of a meal. This recipe is for a thick meat and vegetable soup, which when served with hot French bread and butter, is very satisfying. Although it is excellent followed by Salade Niçoise, it could very well be served with just fruit and cheese.

Salade Niçoise was at one time considered only a summer salad. But now that one can always buy good salad ingredients, it can be made all the year round and can brighten up many a winter meal. Specific quantities and ingredients are given here, but this recipe can always be varied, and almost any combination of ingredients used that you like.

Serve stout with the meal, or perhaps a red Beaujolais wine. Gluwhein would be a good drink to serve before the meal. To make this, heat 1 bottle cheap red wine in a saucepan with 1 pint water, the peeled zest and juice of 2 lemons, 8 cloves and 1 stick of cinnamon. Cover and bring to just below simmering point. Leave for 1 hour. Remove the lemon zest, cloves and cinnamon, and sweeten to taste. A couple of tablespoons of brandy can also be added.

opposite: Pepperpot Beef Soup

Pepperpot Beef Soup

SERVES 4

☆   ① ①   ⊠ ⊠ ⊠

Cooking time:
About 1½ hours

12 oz.-1 lb. shin of beef
2 tablespoons Worcestershire sauce
1 teaspoon salt
1¼ pints [4½ cups] water
2 onions, chopped
2 carrots, sliced in matchsticks
2 sticks celery, sliced
1 bouquet garni
1 tablespoon concentrated tomato purée
1½ oz. noodles or pasta shapes
1 tablespoon butter
2 tablespoons flour

Cut the beef into ½-inch cubes. Place in a bowl with the Worcestershire sauce and marinate for 12 hours in the refrigerator, turning occasionally. Place the meat and sauce in a large pan, add the salt and water and bring slowly to the boil. Add the vegetables, herbs and tomato purée, and simmer until the meat and vegetables are tender, about 45 minutes. Add the pasta and simmer for a further 30 minutes.
Work the butter and flour to a paste. Take the soup off the heat and remove the bouquet garni. Divide the butter paste into three and stir each portion into the soup separately until dissolved. Return the pan to the heat, bring to the boil, and simmer for a further 5 minutes.
Adjust the seasoning, and serve with hot French bread.

Salade Niçoise

SERVES 4

☆   ①   ⊠

1 lettuce
2 large tomatoes
1 green pepper
1 clove garlic, crushed
5 tablespoons French dressing
8 oz. cooked fresh or frozen French beans
¼ cucumber, peeled and diced
2 sticks celery, chopped
2 eggs
7 oz. canned tuna
1¾ oz. canned anchovy fillets
8 black olives

Wash and dry the lettuce and arrange in the bottom and round the sides of a salad bowl. Peel the tomatoes, cut into quarters and remove the pips. Chop the pepper finely, discarding the core and seeds. Add the garlic to the French dressing and mix well. Toss the beans, tomatoes, cucumber, celery and pepper in the French dressing and turn into the salad bowl. *Hard* boil the eggs for 10 minutes. Cool them quickly, shell, and cut them into quarters lengthways. Drain the tuna and anchovies. Arrange the pieces of tuna, anchovy fillets, quartered eggs and olives on top of the salad.

Fresh Fruit and Cheese

Fruit and cheese are an excellent combination and a good simple way to end a meal.
Different fruits make good partners with different cheeses, and it is important to choose both carefully or the flavour of the fruit and the cheese can be spoilt.
Apples go very well with strong flavoured cheeses such as Cheddar, Stilton and Bresse Bleu. Pears on the other hand are better with the milder flavoured cheeses, such as Muenster and Caerphilly. Peaches, strawberries and fresh figs are all 'naturals' with fresh cream or cottage cheese, and so is fresh pineapple. Grapes, however, are one of the few fruits which seem to go well with any cheese, whether strong or mild.
The cheese may be served with biscuits [crackers] and butter, or just on its own with the fruit.

PLANNED AROUND PASTA

Pasta is the basis for many dishes, both simple and elaborate. The Lasagne al Forno given here is a really delicious recipe which makes an excellent family supper dish, or in a larger quantity for a buffet supper party. For a party, a strongly-flavoured red wine would be a good accompaniment.
The Oeufs en Cocotte and Chocolate Cream Mould both complement the main course well, and, like the Lasagne, could also be served for a buffet supper.

opposite: Lasagne al Forno

Oeufs en Cocotte

Baked eggs

SERVES 4

Oven temperature:
Fairly hot 375°F (Gas Mark 5, 190°C)
Cooking time:
About 25 minutes

3 oz. liver sausage or 8 shelled prawns or shrimps
4 tablespoons single [light] cream
4 eggs
salt and pepper
To garnish:
paprika

Lightly butter 4 ramekin dishes. Remove the skin from the liver sausage and cut into 4 slices. Put the liver sausage or prawns into the bottom of the ramekin dishes and spoon over a little of the cream. Stand in a baking tin containing hot water, cover with foil and cook in a fairly hot oven for about 10 minutes to heat the dishes.
Remove from the oven and break an egg into each dish. Spoon over the remaining cream and season with salt and pepper. Return to the oven and bake, uncovered, for a further 15 minutes or until the egg whites are set, but the yolks are still soft.
Serve garnished with a sprinkling of paprika pepper.

Lasagne al Forno

Layers of lasagne pasta, meat sauce and cheese

SERVES 4

Oven temperature:
Fairly hot 375°F (Gas Mark 5, 190°C)
Cooking time:
About 1½ hours

3 tablespoons oil
2 slices bacon, de-rinded and chopped
8 oz. minced [ground] beef
1 large onion, chopped
2 sticks celery, chopped
1 clove garlic, crushed
pinch of mixed dried herbs
salt and freshly milled black pepper
pinch of sugar
2¼ oz. canned concentrated tomato purée
5 fl. oz. water
6 oz. lasagne
½ pint [1¼ cups] Béchamel sauce
3 oz. [¾ cup] grated Gruyère cheese
1 oz. [¼ cup] grated Parmesan cheese

Put 2 tablespoons of the oil into a pan and slowly fry the bacon, beef and onion until brown, stirring frequently. Add the celery, garlic, herbs, seasoning, sugar, tomato purée and water. Cover and simmer gently for about 1 hour, stirring occasionally.
Put the remaining 1 tablespoon oil into a large saucepan with about 2 teaspoons salt and 4 pints water. Bring to the boil and add the lasagne piece by piece. Boil for about 8 minutes or until barely tender. Drain the lasagne, rinse in cold water, then lay out the pieces on a clean, damp cloth (this prevents the pieces of pasta from sticking together).

Put half the meat sauce in the bottom of an ovenproof dish, cover with half the pasta, then half the Béchamel sauce and sprinkle with most of the Gruyère cheese. Repeat these layers, finishing with the sauce. Mix the remaining Gruyère cheese with the Parmesan and sprinkle over the top.
Bake in a fairly hot oven for about 30 minutes or until the top is golden brown.
Serve with a tossed green salad.

Chocolate Cream Mould

SERVES 4

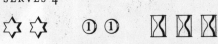

Cooking time:
About 10 minutes

¼ oz. [1 tablespoon] powdered gelatine
2 tablespoons water
2 egg yolks
2 tablespoons castor [fine] sugar
½ pint [1¼ cups] milk
4 oz. plain [semi-sweet] chocolate
¼ teaspoon vanilla essence
5 fl. oz. double [heavy] cream, whipped
To decorate:
chocolate curls

Sprinkle the gelatine over the water and put on one side to soften. Beat the egg yolks and sugar together until thick and creamy. Warm the milk and stir into the egg yolks and sugar. Blend well and strain into the top of a double saucepan, or a basin over hot water. Cook gently, stirring, until the mixture thickens. Break the chocolate into pieces, add to the pan and stir until melted. Remove the top of the double saucepan or the bowl from the heat and stir in the softened gelatine and vanilla essence. Stir until the gelatine has dissolved.
Put in a cold place until the mixture begins to thicken. Fold the cream into the mixture when it is thick but not set. Turn into a very lightly oiled mould and refrigerate until set. To turn out, dip the mould into a bowl of hot water and invert on to a serving plate.
Decorate with chocolate curls.

FRENCH SUPPER

left: Ratatouille
below: Boeuf en Daube

It is sometimes hard to emulate the food one has eaten in a restaurant or on holiday, but with these three uncomplicated recipes, it should not be too difficult.

Ratatouille is almost synonymous with Provence: it is very nearly impossible for anyone to visit that area of France without eating this delicious dish. It is a mixture of onions, aubergines [eggplants], tomatoes, peppers and herbs, stewed slowly in olive oil.

There are many ways of preparing Boeuf en Daube and this is one of the simplest. Originally the name applied to beef cooked in a closed earthenware pot (or daubière) which was buried in hot cinders with hot charcoal added to the top, and left alone to stew gently for a very long time. Now it just applies to a stew or casserole which is cooked very slowly for a long time.

The same wine can be used for cooking the pears and the beef and, although an inexpensive wine can be used, it is best to choose a full-bodied one, such as a Burgundy. A Burgundy would also be the best wine to serve with this meal.

Any wine left over at the end of a meal should be poured into a small screw-topped jar or bottle and can be used for cooking purposes several weeks later.

Ratatouille
Provence-style vegetable stew

SERVES 4-6

Cooking time:
About 1 hour

2 aubergines [eggplants], **diced into ½-inch pieces**
salt
2 onions, finely chopped
4 tablespoons olive oil
2 red or green peppers
4 large tomatoes, peeled and chopped
2 cloves garlic, crushed
12 coriander seeds, crushed
freshly milled black pepper

Put the chopped aubergines into a colander, sprinkle with salt and leave for about 20 minutes for the excess water to drain off. Put the onions into a pan with the oil and cook gently for about 10 minutes or until soft.
Chop the peppers, discarding the cores and seeds and add to the pan with the aubergines. Cover and simmer gently for about 30 minutes.
Add the tomatoes, garlic and coriander and continue cooking for a further 15 minutes. Remove from the heat, adjust seasoning and chill.

Boeuf en Daube
Beef casserole

SERVES 4-6

Cooking time:
About 4 hours
Oven temperature:
Cool 300°F (Gas Mark 1-2, 150°C)

4 onions, sliced
2 carrots, peeled and sliced
2 cloves garlic, crushed
1 bay leaf
sprig rosemary
3 sprigs parsley
2 cloves
salt and pepper
peeled zest ½ orange
2 teaspoons wine vinegar
¾ pint [2 cups] **red wine**
2 lb. chuck steak
2 slices fat bacon

4 tablespoons flour
10 green olives

Put two onions and all the ingredients except the steak, bacon, flour and olives into a shallow dish. Cut the beef into cubes, add to the wine mixture and leave to marinate in the refrigerator, for about 12 hours or longer.
Drain the meat from the marinade. Chop the bacon, put into a heatproof pan and put over a gentle heat until the fat runs. Add the drained meat and remaining onions and brown the meat on all sides. Add the flour and cook until lightly browned. Stir in the strained marinade. Cover and put into a cool oven for about 4 hours. Stone the olives and add to the pan halfway through cooking.
Serve with sauté potatoes, buttered peas and carrots.

Poires au Vin Rouge

Pears in red wine

SERVES 4

Cooking time:
30 minutes

4 oz. [½ cup] sugar
½ pint [1¼ cups] water
¼ teaspoon ground cinnamon
2 tablespoons red currant jelly
8 small ripe pears
½ pint [1¼ cups] red wine

Put the sugar, water, cinnamon and red currant jelly into a saucepan and heat gently until the sugar and jelly have dissolved. Peel the pears, but leave whole with the stalks intact. Put the pears into the saucepan, cover and cook very gently for 15 minutes. Remove the lid, add the wine and cook uncovered for a further 15 minutes.
Remove the pears carefully with a draining spoon and place in a serving dish. Boil the liquid rapidly until it is reduced to a thin syrup. Pour over the pears and chill.
Serve with fresh cream.

The Greeks, like most Mediterranean people, use a great deal of olive oil in their cooking: the Taramasalata is a good example of this. And, like other Eastern Europeans, the Greeks also eat a lot of yogurt, using it extensively in their cooking. In these countries there is a certain mystique about the properties of yogurt, which is associated with longevity.

Taramasalata, or smoked cod's pâté, is now featured on many restaurant menus. Most good fishmongers sell smoked cod's roe, but if you should find it difficult to obtain, a variation of this pâté can be made using cooked fresh cod's roe, with anchovy essence and concentrated tomato purée.

The yogurt marinade for the lamb helps to tenderize the meat, as well as enhance its flavour. The remainder of the marinade also makes a good sauce to serve with the kebabs.

Baklava is as popular in Turkey as it is in Greece. It should be made with phyllo pastry, but as this is very difficult to make and can only be bought in specialist Greek and Turkish shops, the recipe given here is a simplified version using puff pastry.

To give a final Greek touch to the meal, you could serve a bottle of Retsina wine with it.

GREEK SUPPER

Taramasalata
Smoked cod's roe paté

SERVES 4

8 oz. smoked cod's roe
3 slices bread
1 clove garlic, crushed
8 tablespoons olive oil
2 tablespoons lemon juice
freshly milled black pepper

Remove the skin from the roe and mash in a bowl until smooth, or pound in a pestle and mortar. Remove the crusts from the bread and soak in cold water. *Squeeze* out as much water as possible and add to the cod's roe with the garlic, pounding it well. Gradually add the oil, a teaspoon at a time, and the lemon juice. Season to taste with the pepper.
Serve with hot toast and butter.

Shish Kebabs
Cubes of meat and vegetables marinated in yogurt and herb sauce

SERVES 4

Cooking time:
About 20 minutes

$\frac{1}{2}$ pint [$1\frac{1}{4}$ cups] tomato juice
2 teaspoons made mustard
5 fl. oz. natural yogurt
2 teaspoons finely chopped mint
1 tablespoon chopped chives
$\frac{1}{4}$ teaspoon ground cinnamon
salt and freshly milled black pepper
1 lb. lean lamb from the leg
1 aubergine [eggplant]
1 green pepper
2 large tomatoes, sliced
8 small onions, par-boiled
2 tablespoons oil

Mix together the tomato juice, mustard, yogurt, herbs, cinnamon and seasoning, and put into a dish. Cut the lamb into 1-inch cubes. Put these into the sauce and leave to marinate for about 5 hours, turning occasionally.
Cut the aubergine into thick slices, sprinkle with salt and leave for about 30 minutes for the excess water to drain off. Remove and discard the core

and seeds from the pepper; cut the flesh into 8 pieces. Divide the cubes of meat, aubergine, pepper and tomato slices and onions among four skewers. Brush the vegetables but not the meat with the oil. Put the kebabs over a barbecue or under a hot grill and cook for about 20 minutes. Brush the meat with the yogurt sauce from time to time during cooking and brush the vegetables with the oil.
Serve any remaining sauce with the kebabs, and boiled rice.

Baklava
Honey, almond and pastry layers

SERVES 4-6

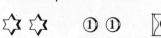

Oven temperature:
Fairly hot 400°F (Gas Mark 6, 200°C)
Cooking time:
About 20 minutes

6 oz. [1 cup] blanched almonds
4 tablespoons butter
3 tablespoons honey
$\frac{1}{2}$ teaspoon ground cinnamon
13 oz. packet puff pastry, defrosted
8 oz. [1 cup] sugar
$\frac{1}{2}$ pint [$1\frac{1}{4}$ cups] water
1 tablespoon lemon juice

Chop the almonds finely. Cream the butter, 1 tablespoon of the honey and the cinnamon together. Stir in the chopped nuts.
Roll out the pastry and cut out 4 × 6-inch squares. Cover a baking sheet with foil, and add one square of pastry spreading this with one third of the nut mixture. Top with another pastry square, and more nuts, and continue these layers finishing with a square of pastry. Mark the top layer into diamonds. Put into a fairly hot oven and bake for about 20 minutes, or until the top is golden brown.
While the pastry is cooking, put the sugar, water, lemon juice and the remaining honey into a saucepan. Heat slowly until the sugar dissolves. Bring to the boil and simmer for 5 minutes.
Take the baking sheet from the oven, and remove the foil and baklava together. Pull up the foil to form a case around the sides of the pastry. Pour the hot syrup over it, and leave to soak.
When it is cold cut into diamonds and serve with cream.

above: Shish Kebabs
right: Taramasalata
far right: Baklava

left: *frying the Churros*
below: *Gazpacho Andaluz and Paella*

SPANISH SUPPER

Gazpacho, Paella and Churros are all traditional Spanish dishes, although the first two vary slightly in their ingredients in different parts of Spain.

Gazpacho is one of the most famous of the world's cold soups, and with good reason. It is a basic tomato purée flavoured with cucumber, peppers, onion, garlic and olive oil, and should be served with ice cubes floating on the top. Although it can be served at any time during the year, it is of course ideal on a hot summer's day.

Paella means 'cooked in a pan', and the true Spanish Paella should be cooked and served in one pan, known as a 'paellara'. This should not be difficult with the cast iron oven-to-table ware which most people have today, but if you do not possess a suitable dish it can be cooked in a large saucepan and turned on to a heated plate.

Churros, or fried ribbons of choux pastry, are served in Spain on festive occasions, and make a traditional ending to the meal. Fresh peaches or oranges would be a good alternative.

Serve either a Spanish red wine, or a chilled dry sherry, throughout.

Gazpacho Andaluz
Iced tomato soup with garlic

SERVES 4-6

1 green pepper
2 lb. tomatoes, peeled
2 cloves garlic
1 medium-sized onion
½ cucumber, peeled
2 oz. [⅔ cup] white or brown breadcrumbs
2 tablespoons red wine vinegar
5 fl. oz. chicken stock
6 tablespoons olive oil
salt and pepper

Core the pepper and discard the seeds. Put with the tomatoes, garlic, onion, and cucumber into a blender, or chop the pepper, onions and cucumber finely, rub the tomatoes through a sieve, and crush the garlic. Add the breadcrumbs, vinegar, stock and oil and season to taste. Chill.
Add ice cubes to the soup, and serve with toasted bread croûtons and chopped cucumber.

Paella
Rice dish with chicken and seafood

SERVES 4

Cooking time:
About 30 minutes

1 quart fresh mussels
salt and pepper
1 green or red pepper
4 chicken drumsticks
1 large onion, chopped
2 tablespoons olive oil
5 oz. [1 cup] long-grain rice
1 chicken stock cube
large pinch saffron powder
4 oz. shelled prawns or shrimps
4 oz. garlic sausage, sliced
To garnish:
black olives
4 oz. unshelled prawns, cooked

Rinse the mussels and scrub well. Discard any that do not close when sharply tapped; these are not safe to eat. Put the mussels into a pan with salt, pepper and water to cover. Simmer gently until they open, about 5 minutes. Discard any that do not open. Remove the mussels from their shells, reserving about 8 in their shells for garnish. Retain the liquid.
Chop the pepper, discarding the core and seeds. Fry the chicken, onion and pepper in the oil for about 5 minutes. Add the rice, chicken stock cube, saffron, seasoning and mussel liquid made up to ¾ pint [2 cups] with water. Simmer gently over a low heat for about 20 minutes.
Stir in the shelled prawns, garlic sausage and mussels. Cook for a further 5 minutes, adding a little extra water if it looks too dry.
Serve garnished with the reserved mussels, olives and unshelled prawns.

Churros
Fried choux pastries

SERVES 4

Cooking time:
About 8 minutes

2½ oz. choux pastry (see page 54)
deep oil or fat for frying
sieved icing [confectioners'] sugar

Make up the choux pastry and allow to cool. Put into a piping bag with a ½-inch plain nozzle.
Heat the oil to 350°F or so that a cube of day-old bread turns golden brown in 1 minute. Holding the piping bag in your left hand, squeeze out 8-inch lengths of the pastry into the hot fat. Cut off the lengths with a pair of scissors held in the right hand. Do not cook more than 2 or 3 lengths at a time.
Fry the pastries for about 8 minutes or until crisp and golden brown on both sides. Remove from the pan, drain, and serve liberally sprinkled with icing [confectioners'] sugar.
They are better served hot, but may also be eaten cold: in this case, sprinkle with icing sugar when they have cooled.

The Italians are well known for their veal dishes and use this meat more than any other. Osso Bucco, a traditional Italian veal stew, is made from the knuckle with the marrow carefully preserved. It is cooked very slowly in the oven with tomatoes, carrots, onions, celery and white wine, so that the meat is really tender and the maximum flavour is extracted from the bones.

Aubergines can be stuffed in a variety of ways and can be served as a first, or as a main course. The stuffing given here is a little unusual, and includes Ricotta cheese, but any sort of cream cheese may be substituted. The aubergines can be served hot, but are better served lightly chilled.

Zabaglione is probably the best known Italian dessert. It is a rich egg custard which can be served warm or chilled, on its own, or poured over fruit. It is particularly good with peaches and pears.

White chianti would be an obvious choice of wine to serve and a selection of cheeses—including if possible Gorgonzola or Dolcelatte, and Bel Paese—would complete the meal. For a simpler supper the aubergines and Zabaglione could be omitted, and fresh peaches or pears with cheese could be served instead.

Melanzane Ripiene
Stuffed aubergines [eggplants]

SERVES 4

Oven temperature:
Fairly hot 400°F (Gas Mark 6, 200°C)
Cooking time:
40 minutes

2 aubergines [eggplants]
salt
about 4 tablespoons oil

5-6 mushrooms, finely chopped
1 onion, finely chopped
2 oz. Ricotta, or other full fat soft cheese
2 oz. [⅔ cup] soft breadcrumbs
1 large tomato, peeled and chopped
freshly milled black pepper
1 tablespoon grated Parmesan cheese

Cut the aubergines in half lengthways. Score the flesh with a knife, sprinkle with salt and leave for 30 minutes for the excess water to drain off. Then brush with oil, and grill [broil] slowly for about 20 minutes. Remove the aubergine pulp, and chop this finely. *Fry* the mushrooms and onions gently in 1½ tablespoons oil. Mix the cream cheese with half of the breadcrumbs. Add the peeled and chopped tomato with the mushrooms, onions and aubergine pulp to the cream cheese mixture. Mix well, and season to taste with the black pepper. Spoon the mixture into the aubergine cases. Sprinkle with the remaining breadcrumbs mixed with the Parmesan cheese, and add a little oil to moisten. Bake in a fairly hot oven for about 20 minutes.
Serve chilled.

Osso Bucco
Veal-bone stew

SERVES 4.

Oven temperature:
Warm 325°F (Gas Mark 3, 170°C)
Cooking time:
About 3 hours

2-2½ lb. knuckle of veal or use 1½ lb. stewing veal
2 tablespoons olive oil
3 carrots, peeled and sliced
2 sticks celery, chopped
1 onion, chopped
2 tablespoons flour
5 fl. oz. dry white wine
1 clove garlic, crushed
½ pint [1¼ cups] water
1 chicken stock cube
14 oz. canned tomatoes
1 sprig parsley
1 bay leaf
salt and pepper
To garnish:
grated zest ½ lemon
2 tablespoon coarsely chopped parsley
½ clove garlic, crushed

Ask the butcher to cut the knuckle into 1½-2 inch pieces or the stewing veal into 1½-inch cubes. Heat the oil in a large pan, and fry half the meat at a time over a moderate heat, turning it once, until brown. Drain, and put into a casserole.
Add the carrots, celery and onion to the pan and cook gently for 5 minutes. Sprinkle the flour over them, and continue cooking, stirring occasionally until the flour is browned. Then blend in the wine, garlic, water, stock cube, tomatoes, parsley, bay leaf and salt and pepper. Bring to the boil, and pour the mixture over the meat.
Cover the casserole and put it into a warm oven for about 2½ hours, or until the veal is tender. Taste, and if necessary adjust the seasoning. Mix together the lemon zest, parsley and garlic, and sprinkle this over the veal before serving.
Serve with saffron rice and salad.

Zabaglione
Whipped egg yolks, marsala and sugar

SERVES 4

3 egg yolks
4 oz. castor [½ cup fine] sugar
4-6 tablespoons Marsala

Put the egg yolks, sugar and Marsala into a mixing bowl and mix lightly. Now put the bowl over a saucepan of boiling water, but draw the pan off the stove. The mixture needs a very gentle heat. Whisk until it is thick and fluffy.
Pour into four glasses, and serve either warm or cold.

ITALIAN SUPPER

right: Osso Bucco
below: Zabaglione

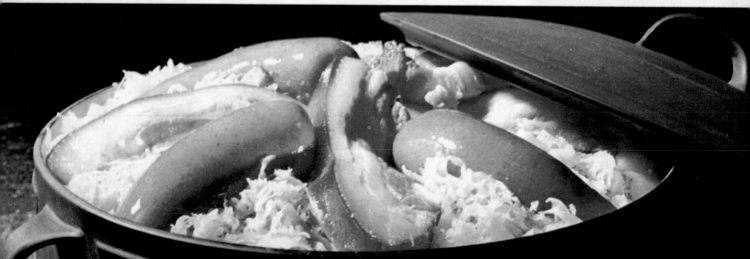

opposite:
far left: Schwarzwalder-Torte
left: Bismarck Hering Salat
bottom: Sauerkraut mit Knackwurst

German food is sometimes thought rather heavy. Although some of their food (particularly the dumplings) is rather stodgy, this is by no means the case with all of it.

For a family supper you might serve lager with this meal, and leave out the gâteau. For a more special occasion, though, serve either a real German beer or a chilled dry white wine.

The Germans (like the Scandinavians) generally serve their herrings pickled, and the appetizing first course is simple to prepare.

Nowadays it is quite easy to buy cans or jars of sauerkraut in good grocers and delicatessens. In some delicatessens the sauerkraut is sold from a large wooden keg or barrel. (If you do buy it like this, it is a good idea to put the sauerkraut into a colander and rinse it in cold water to remove the excess salt). Although knackwurst or frankfurters have been given here, you can use any sort of sausage you wish. If your family like black pudding, this would go very well with the sauerkraut.

The Black Forest Gâteau is a really delicious rich gâteau made from puff pastry, chocolate cake, cherries and cream, flavoured with kirsch. If you do not have any kirsch, substitute brandy, cherry brandy, or dry vermouth.

Bismarck Hering Salat
Bismarck herring salad

SERVES 4

12 oz. jar Bismarck or luncheon herrings
5 fl. oz. sour cream, or 5 fl. oz. double [heavy] cream mixed with 1 tablespoon lemon juice
salt and freshly milled black pepper
To garnish:
watercress

Drain the herrings and the onions which are packed with them, from the liquid in the jar. Cut the herrings into bite-sized pieces. Mix most of the herrings and onions with the sour cream, and season to taste. Turn on to a plate. Garnish with the watercress, and the reserved herring and onion pieces. *Serve* with a dark or rye bread.

Sauerkraut mit Knackwurst
Bavarian sauerkraut with bacon and frankfurters

SERVES 4

Oven temperature:
Fairly hot 375°F (Gas Mark 5, 190°C)
Cooking time:
About 1 hour

1 large cooking apple
2 carrots
4 tablespoons butter, melted
1 lb. canned or jar sauerkraut
1 teaspoon caraway seeds
freshly milled black pepper
4 thick slices streaky or flank bacon
4 knackwurst or 8 frankfurter sausages

Peel, core and grate the apple. Peel and grate the carrots. Put the apple, carrots, butter, sauerkraut, caraway seeds and pepper into a bowl, and mix well. Turn this into a casserole, and top with the bacon. Cover and bake in a fairly hot oven for 45 minutes. Arrange the sausages on top and bake uncovered for a further 15 minutes.
Serve with floury boiled potatoes.

Schwarzwälder-Torte
Black Forest gâteau

SERVES 8

Oven temperature:
Very hot 450°F (Gas Mark 8, 230°C)
Fairly hot 375°F (Gas Mark 5, 190°C)
Cooking time:
About 30 minutes

$7\frac{1}{2}$ oz. packet puff pastry, defrosted
3 large eggs
6 oz. castor [$\frac{3}{4}$ cup fine] sugar
$\frac{1}{4}$ teaspoon vanilla essence
5 tablespoons self-raising flour, or plain flour mixed with $\frac{1}{2}$ teaspoon baking powder
1 tablespoon cocoa
1 tablespoon hot water
14 oz. canned cherry pie filling
$\frac{1}{2}$ pint double [$1\frac{1}{4}$ cups heavy] cream, whipped
4 tablespoons kirsch
2 oz. plain [semi-sweet] chocolate, grated

Roll out the pastry and cut out an $8\frac{1}{2}$-inch circle. Put on to a damp baking sheet and bake in a very hot oven for about 12-15 minutes or until golden brown. Remove from the oven and cool. Whisk eggs, 4 ounces [$\frac{1}{2}$ cup] sugar and the vanilla essence together until thick and creamy, and until the whisk leaves a trail when lifted out.
Sift together the flour, baking powder, if used, and cocoa. Fold these into the egg mixture carefully, and then fold in the water as well. Turn into two greased and lined 8-inch diameter tins and bake in a fairly hot oven for about 15 minutes, or until the cakes spring back when touched. Turn out and cool.
Fold the kirsch and the remaining amount of sugar into the lightly whipped cream. Spread the puff pastry with about a quarter of the cream then cover with half the cherry pie filling. Put one of the layers on top, and trim the edges of the puff pastry to match.
Spread the cake with another quarter of the cream and the remaining cherry pie filling. Top with the second chocolate sponge and put on a serving plate. Spread the remaining cream over the top and sides of the cake. Sprinkle with grated chocolate. Chill and serve.

43

SCANDINAVIAN SUPPER

Smørrebrød, or open sandwiches, are probably the first Scandinavian foods most people think of. There are in fact a great many other traditional and popular dishes from this area. The three recipes here are really Danish, but are also found in the other Scandinavian countries.

Danish caviare (lumpfish roe) always sounds very luxurious and extravagant, but it is not as expensive as many people imagine. Mixed with lemon juice and garnished with hard-boiled egg, it is an excellent and quickly prepared first course.
Frikadeller, or meat balls, are popular in all the Scandinavian countries. The recipe given here is a basic one; you will find that they are served in a great many other ways.

The Danish Apple Charlotte is also sometimes known by the rather attractive name of Peasant Girl with Veil. It should be assembled about 2 hours before serving so that it is lightly chilled.

This menu can make a good family supper without the first course, but with the caviare it is an excellent supper to serve when entertaining. A Danish lager, beer or a light red wine would go very well with it.

Caviare Forret
Danish caviare hors d'oeuvre

SERVES 4

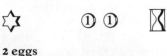

2 eggs
2 × 3 oz. jars lumpfish roe
juice 1 lemon

Hard boil the eggs for 10 minutes. Run them under cold water, shell, and slice. Mix the lumpfish roe with the lemon juice, and pile on to a serving dish. Decorate with the hard-boiled egg slices.
Serve with Danish rye bread, or any brown or rye bread, and butter.

Frikadeller
Danish meat balls

SERVES 4-6

Cooking time:
About 10 minutes

12 oz. minced [ground] beef
12 oz. minced [ground] pork
3 tablespoons flour
½ teaspoon salt
freshly milled black pepper
¼ teaspoon ground allspice
1 small onion, grated
5 fl. oz. milk
1 egg, beaten
4 tablespoons butter
1 tablespoon oil

Mix the meat with the flour, salt, pepper, allspice and onion. Gradually beat in the milk and egg.
Using two tablespoons, shape the mixture into oval balls. Heat the butter and oil in a frying pan, and fry the meat balls gently on all sides until they are golden brown.
Drain them, and serve hot with caramelized potatoes and red cabbage.

Note: To caramelize potatoes heat 2 tablespoons of sugar in a frying pan until it just melts. Add 4 tablespoons butter, when this has melted mix it with the sugar. Toss 1½ pounds of cooked new potatoes in the sugar and butter, and heat gently until the potatoes are golden brown.

Aeblekage
Danish apple charlotte

SERVES 4

Cooking time:
About 20 minutes

1½ lb. cooking apples
grated zest 1 lemon
2 tablespoons water
4 tablespoons sugar
4 oz. [½ cup] butter
6 oz. [2 cups] white breadcrumbs
4 tablespoons light brown sugar
5 fl. oz. double [heavy] cream, whipped
2 oz. chocolate, coarsely grated

Peel, core and slice the apples, and put them into a saucepan with the lemon zest, water and white sugar. Cover, and cook until the apples are soft, then mash to a smooth purée. Leave to cool.
Melt the butter in a large frying pan and gently fry the breadcrumbs until crisp and golden. Add the brown sugar and allow to cool.
Put half the apple purée into the bottom of a glass dish, add half the crumbs, and then the remaining apple purée and the rest of the crumbs. Spread the lightly whipped cream over the top, and sprinkle on the grated chocolate.
Serve lightly chilled.

opposite:
top: Aeblekage
bottom: Frikadeller

44

FIRST COURSES

The five hors d'oeuvres on these two pages are rather luxurious ones. Four of them are served cold as people generally find cold ones easier (especially when entertaining): all the preparation can be done in advance and there is no last minute fuss.

from left to right:
Country Pâté, Iced Carrot Soup, Buckling and Lemon Pâté, Smoked Trout Mousse, Creamy Topped Scallops

The Country Pâté is a good, rough French terrine. It is excellent served as a start to a buffet party, or it could make a main course if served with salad. It freezes very well so you may like to make up the large quantity given here and freeze half of it, or freeze it in quantities large enough for two or four for supper.

Buckling Pâté make a rather unusual, and delicious fish pâté. Buckling, a form of smoked herring, can be obtained from most good fishmongers and some delicatessens. As it is a smoked fish, this pâté will keep well for several days in the refrigerator.

Smoked Trout Mousse provides a light first course which would be excellent served before a rather rich main course or on a hot summer's day.

Iced Carrot Soup is an inexpensive soup which can be served at any time during the year. It could also be served hot; add the cream after sieving the soup, and reheat gently without boiling.

The Creamy Topped Scallops can be made with fresh or frozen scallops. The whole dish can be completely prepared in advance and left in the refrigerator until you wish to grill it. If you do this, however, the grilling time should be slightly increased.

Country Pâté

SERVES 10-12

Oven temperature:
Warm 325°F (Gas Mark 3, 170°C)
Cooking time:
$2\frac{1}{2}$ hours

2 bay leaves
4 slices streaky bacon, de-rinded
6 oz. [2 cups] white breadcrumbs
2 eggs
5 fl. oz. port
2 cloves garlic, crushed
8 oz. fresh belly of pork
8 oz. bacon trimmings
1 lb. pig's liver
1 lb. chickens' livers
$\frac{1}{2}$ teaspoon dried thyme
$\frac{1}{2}$ teaspoon mixed dried herbs
$1\frac{1}{2}$ teaspoons grated nutmeg
3 teaspoons salt
$\frac{1}{2}$ teaspoon freshly milled black pepper

Well grease a 3-pint terrine or loaf tin. Arrange the bay leaves on the bottom. Stretch the bacon with the back of a knife on a board and line the base of the dish with it.
Mix together the breadcrumbs, eggs, port and garlic. Finely mince the pork belly and bacon trimmings, discarding any rind, and the livers. Add to the bread with the remaining ingredients, and mix well.
Turn into the prepared terrine or tin, and cover with a double layer of foil and the lid. Put into a baking tin containing 2-inches of hot water, and bake in a warm oven for $2\frac{1}{2}$ hours. Remove from the oven and allow to cool, then chill. The finished appearance will be improved if you can put heavy weights on the foil-topped pâté, while it is cooling.
Turn out, and serve with hot toast or French bread and butter.

Buckling and Lemon Pâté

SERVES 4

1 large buckling
4 oz. [$\frac{1}{2}$ cup] butter, softened
1 tablespoon lemon juice
1 clove garlic, crushed
freshly milled black pepper
To garnish:
slice of lemon

Drop the buckling into boiling water for 1 minute. Drain, then skin and bone. Pound the flesh with a wooden spoon, or with a pestle and mortar, and blend in the softened butter. Alternatively, put the buckling and butter into a blender.
Add the lemon juice and garlic, and season to taste with the pepper. Turn into a small dish and garnish with a twist of lemon.
Serve with hot toast, or French bread and butter.

Variation:
A smoked trout may be used in place of the buckling.

Note: Buckling are also delicious on their own, served with horseradish flavoured cream.

Smoked Trout Mousse

SERVES 4-6

☆ ① ① ⊠

2 smoked trout
2 tablespoons butter, softened
juice ½ lemon
salt and freshly milled black pepper
pinch cayenne pepper
½ pint double [1¼ cups heavy] cream,
  whipped
To garnish:
lemon and cucumber slices

Skin and bone the trout. Pound the
flesh with a wooden spoon or with a
pestle and mortar. Add the softened
butter and the lemon juice. Mix well
and season to taste with the salt, black
pepper and cayenne pepper. Fold in
the cream. Turn into a dish and chill.
Decorate with lemon and cucumber
slices, and serve with thinly sliced
brown bread and butter.

Note: For a special occasion the
mousse could be decorated with rolls
of smoked salmon, as shown in the
photograph.

Iced Carrot Soup

SERVES 4

☆ ① ⊠ ⊠ ⊠

Cooking time:
About 1 hour

2 tablespoons butter or margarine
1 lb. carrots, peeled and sliced
1 large onion, chopped
1 leek, chopped (optional)
1 pint [2½ cups] water
1 chicken stock cube
salt and pepper
1 teaspoon sugar
4 tablespoons single [light] cream
1 tablespoon chopped chives

Heat the butter or margarine in a pan
and fry the carrots, onion and leek for
about 5 minutes. Add the water, stock
cube and seasoning. Cover and simmer
gently for about 1 hour. Remove the
pan from the heat and either rub
through a sieve or put into a blender.
Add the sugar and 3 tablespoons cream.
Adjust the seasoning and chill.
Just before serving, spoon over the
remaining cream to form an attractive
pattern, sprinkle with chives, and put
a few ice cubes into the soup.

Variation:
Halve the quantity of carrots, and add
½ pound of young turnips, peeled and
sliced. Garnish the finished soup with
mixed chives and parsley, chopped.

Creamy Topped Scallops

SERVES 4

☆ ☆ ① ① ① ⊠

Cooking time:
About 20 minutes

8 scallops
1 small onion, chopped
½ pint [1¼ cups] dry white wine
2 tablespoons butter
2 tablespoons flour
5 fl. oz. milk
salt and freshly milled black pepper
1 tablespoon grated Parmesan
  cheese
4 tablespoons double [heavy] cream,
  whipped

Wash the scallops thoroughly, and
remove all the black threads and grit.
Put the scallops, onion and wine into a
saucepan. Simmer until the scallops
become opaque, about 10 minutes.
Remove the scallops and onions with a
perforated spoon. Now reduce the
wine to 2½ fl. oz. by boiling it fast in the
pan. (Do not cover it at this stage.)
Melt the butter in a pan, stir
in the flour, and cook for 1 minute.
Gradually stir in the milk and the
wine. Add the scallops and the chopped
onion, and season to taste. Spoon the
mixture into scallop shells or ramekins.
Fold the cheese into the cream and
spread evenly over the scallops.
Grill until golden brown, and serve at
once.

Variation:
Shrimps can be treated in the same way:
use 4 ounces of frozen shelled shrimps,
or ½ lb. unshelled shrimps. If using
unshelled shrimps, shell them, and
simmer the shells in the wine for about
15 minutes. Strain and reduce the wine
to 2½ fl. oz. as above. If using frozen
shelled shrimps, simmer the wine with
the chopped onion and a sprig of parsley
then reduce as above.

FIVE MAIN COURSES

Rabbit is very cheap, and cooked with a little imagination can also be very good. Try lightly toasting French bread, spreading it with butter and a little French mustard, and serving it on the top of the Rabbit Stew.

Pork and cider always combine well, and the Somerset Pork is no exception; a serving suggestion to add an extra bite to its flavour is also given.

The Vol-au-Vent Special is a chicken or turkey vol-au-vent with salted peanuts and raisins added to the sauce. If you have any stock, replace half of the milk with this. For a quick supper, buy 4-6 ready-made vol-au-vent cases, heat, and spoon the sauce into them.

The filling for the Creamy Veal Pie is given a slight piquancy with the addition of lemon zest as the veal is cooking. The pastry is decorated in a rather unusual way by topping it with lattice strips of pastry, cut out with a pastry wheel.

The Herby Beef Loaf is excellent, either served hot with a tomato sauce and vegetables, or cold with thick mayonnaise and salad.

opposite: French Rabbit Stew Somerset Pork and Saute Potatoes

French Rabbit Stew

SERVES 4-6

Cooking time:
About 1 hour

4-6 rabbit pieces
salt and pepper
4 slices bacon
1 lb. small onions
2 tablespoons butter or margarine
4 tablespoons flour
5 fl. oz. water
5 fl. oz. red wine
4 oz. mushrooms
1 clove garlic, crushed
2 bay leaves

Wash the rabbit joints well, and dry them. Season each with the salt and pepper. Remove the rind from the bacon, and cut into small pieces. Peel the onions, and leave them whole. *Melt* the butter or margarine in a saucepan and add the bacon and onions. Fry lightly until golden brown, then remove from the pan, and add the rabbit joints. Fry these for 5 minutes, or until they are brown, and remove from the pan. Stir in the flour and cook over a gentle heat for about 10 minutes, stirring from time to time until it becomes a rich brown colour. *Remove* from the heat and gradually stir in the water and wine. Return to the heat, bring to the boil, stirring all the time and cook for 1 minute. Return the rabbit, bacon and onions to the pan with the mushrooms, garlic and bay leaves. Bring to the boil, cover, and simmer for about 45 minutes. *Remove* the bay leaves before serving, and accompany the rabbit with creamed potatoes and buttered carrots.

Somerset Pork

SERVES 4-6

Cooking time:
About 1¾ hours

1½ lb. lean pork
2 oz. [½ cup] flour
salt and pepper

4 tablespoons dripping or margarine
2 onions, chopped
2 sticks celery, chopped
1 pint [2½ cups] dry cider
4 carrots, peeled and chopped

Cut the meat into 1½-inch cubes. *Mix* the flour with salt and pepper and put into a plastic or brown paper bag. Add the meat, and toss it in the seasoned flour. Heat the dripping or margarine in a pan and fry the meat, onions and celery until lightly brown. Add any flour remaining in the bag. Gradually stir in the cider and bring to the boil, stirring well. Add the carrots, and then cover the pan and simmer gently for about 1½ hours, or until the meat is tender. Taste, and adjust the seasoning. *Serve* with creamed potatoes and sprigs of cauliflower.

Note: 5 fl. oz. yogurt can be added to the stew at the end of cooking. Do not re-boil after the yogurt is added.

Vol-au-Vent Special

with peanuts and raisins

SERVES 4-6

Oven temperature:
Very hot 450°F (Gas Mark 8, 230°C)
Cooking time:
20 minutes

1 × 13 oz packet puff pastry, defrosted
1 pint [2½ cups] milk
4 oz. [½ cup] butter or margarine
1 medium-sized onion, finely chopped
6 slices streaky bacon, de-rinded and chopped
6-8 mushrooms, thinly sliced
2 oz. [½ cup] flour
8 oz. [1 cup] cooked chicken or turkey, roughly chopped
2 oz. [¼ cup] salted peanuts
2 oz. [⅓ cup] seedless raisins
salt and pinch cayenne pepper

Roll out the pastry to a 9-inch square. Trim the edges and knock these up with the back of a knife. Place the square carefully on a baking tray, and mark a square 1 inch from the edge. Cut half-way through the pastry along this line. Make a criss-cross pattern over the whole of the top with a knife. Brush with a little milk, and bake in a very hot oven for 12 minutes. Remove the marked square to use as a lid, and place on a separate baking tray. Place both trays in the oven for a further 8 minutes.

Melt half of the butter or margarine in a pan and fry the onion, bacon and mushrooms for about 10 minutes. Melt the remaining amount of the butter or margarine in a separate pan, add the flour and cook for 1 minute. Gradually stir in the milk and bring to the boil, stirring all the time. Add the bacon mixture to the white sauce with the chicken or turkey, peanuts, and raisins. Season to taste with the salt and cayenne pepper.

Put the hot sauce mixture into the hot puff pastry case and top with the lid. *Serve* with green beans or buttered courgettes [zucchini].

Creamy Veal Pie

SERVES 4

Oven temperature:
Fairly hot 400°F (Gas Mark 6, 200°C)
Cooking time:
1 hour 20 minutes

1 lb. stewing veal
2 tablespoons butter or margarine
½ pint [1¼ cups] water
peeled zest of ½ lemon
pinch mixed dried herbs
1 onion, peeled and quartered
salt and pepper
1 tablespoon cornflour [cornstarch]
2 oz. button mushrooms
4 tablespoons single [light] cream
6 oz. short crust pastry (see page 54)
1 egg, beaten

Cut the veal into 1-inch cubes. Heat the butter or margarine in a pan, and fry the veal quickly on all sides, to seal. Pour over the water, and add the lemon zest together with the herbs, onion and seasoning. Cover and simmer for 1 hour.

Blend the cornflour with 2 tablespoons water. Remove the veal from the heat, and stir in the cornflour. Return to the heat and bring to the boil, stirring all the time. Simmer for 2 minutes, then take off the heat, and remove the lemon peel. Stir in the cream and mushrooms. Turn into a 2-pint pie dish and allow to cool.

Make up the short crust pastry. Roll it out and cut a strip ½-inch wide, to go round the edge of the pie dish. Brush the edge of the pie dish with beaten egg and lay the strip on top. Brush the pastry strip with the egg, and lay the rolled out pastry over the top of the pie. Trim the edges, and press with the prongs of a fork to decorate. Roll the pastry trimmings out thinly and, using a pastry wheel if you have one, cut it into long thin strips. Brush the top of the pie with beaten egg and lattice the strips over the top: brush these with beaten egg. Bake in a fairly hot oven for about 20 minutes, or until the pastry is golden brown.

Serve with potatoes baked in their jackets, and buttered carrots or spinach.

Herby Beef Loaf

SERVES 4-6

Oven temperature:
Moderate 350°F (Gas Mark 4, 180°C)
Cooking time:
1½ hours

1 lb. minced [ground] beef
8 oz. pork sausagemeat
2 oz. [⅔ cup] white breadcrumbs
1 onion, grated
1 tablespoon chopped parsley
1 tablespoon chopped chives
½ teaspoon fresh chopped or
  ¼ teaspoon dried sage
2 teaspoons Worcestershire sauce
salt and freshly milled black pepper
2 eggs, beaten

Mix all the ingredients together, and bind with the beaten eggs. Turn this into a well-greased 2-lb. loaf tin and cover with foil. Now put the tin into a larger baking tin or dish, which contains about an inch of cold water. Bake in a moderate oven for 1½ hours.

Either turn out and serve hot with a tomato sauce or allow it to cool in the tin. Then turn out, and serve with thick mayonnaise.

opposite: Creamy Veal Pie
Vol-au-Vent Special
Herby Beef Loaf with Tomato Sauce

FIVE DESSERTS AND SAVOURIES

Savouries are not often served these days, perhaps because our meals are no longer very formal occasions. But Welsh Rarebit is still a very popular dish; we give it here with the warning that it is very filling, and so should not be served after a very heavy main course. A bowl of soup followed by Welsh Rarebit would make an excellent winter's meal.

If one member of your family is particularly fond of Welsh Rarebit, the mixture can be made up and stored in a plastic box in the refrigerator for about a week. All you then have to do is to spread enough for one portion on to a piece of toast, and grill it.

Apple Pan Dowdy is an American dessert which, coupled with traditional British Queen of Puddings, provides a delicious and homey element.

Profiteroles and Crème Brûlée are rather more elegant desserts. When making the Crème Brûleé, care must be taken that the custard does not boil, as this will make it curdle. Because the recipe contains only cream and egg yolks (and so has a very high fat content), it will freeze very successfully. The choux buns for the Profiteroles also freeze extremely well, filled or empty, and are excellent to have available so that this rather luxurious dessert can be made in no time.

Welsh Rarebit

SERVES 4

☆　①　🖾

Cooking time:
About 10 minutes

2 tablespoons butter
2 teaspoons flour
¼ teaspoon dry mustard
4 tablespoons milk
2 tablespoons ale (or use 2 more tablespoons milk)
8 oz. [2 cups] grated Cheddar cheese
1-2 teaspoons Worcestershire sauce
salt and freshly milled black pepper
4 slices buttered toast

Heat the butter in a pan, stir in the flour and mustard, and cook for a minute, stirring all the time. Gradually stir in the milk and the ale, if used. Add the cheese and Worcestershire sauce, and stir over a low heat until the cheese has melted. Season to taste with salt and pepper.
Spoon the mixture on to buttered toast, and grill [broil] until golden brown.

Note: It is a good idea to cover the rack on the grill pan with foil, before grilling the rarebits. This will prevent any of the cheese, which may run from burning on the pan.

Variations:
§ **Buck Rarebit**
Top each rarebit with a poached egg.

§ **York Rarebit**
Add a slice of ham to each slice of buttered toast, then add the rarebit mixture and grill [broil] as before.

Apple Pan Dowdy

SERVES 4

☆　①　🖾 🖾

Oven temperature:
Fairly hot 375°F (Gas Mark 5, 190°C)
Cooking time:
55 minutes

3 large cooking apples
2 tablespoons brown sugar
1 tablespoon golden [corn] syrup
¼ teaspoon grated nutmeg
¼ teaspoon ground cinnamon
4 oz. [1 cup] self-raising flour, or plain flour mixed with 1 teaspoon baking powder
pinch salt
4 tablespoons sugar
1 egg, beaten
4 tablespoons milk
4 tablespoons butter or margarine, melted

Peel, core and thinly slice the cooking apples. Put into a 1½-pint ovenproof dish with the brown sugar, syrup, nutmeg and cinnamon. Cover with foil, and bake for about 20 minutes until the apples are almost soft. Sift the flour, salt, and the baking powder, if used. Add the sugar, egg, milk and butter or margarine and beat well together. Spoon this mixture on top of the apples, and spread evenly. Return to the oven and bake uncovered for a further 30-35 minutes.
Turn upside down on to a serving dish, and serve with fresh cream.

Queen of Puddings

SERVES 4

Oven temperature:
Moderate 350°F (Gas Mark 4, 180°C)
Cooking time:
40-50 minutes

¾ pint [2 cups] milk
2 tablespoons butter
grated zest ½ lemon
2 eggs, separated
4 oz. castor [½ cup fine] sugar
3 oz. [1 cup] breadcrumbs
2 tablespoons raspberry jam

Heat the milk, butter and lemon zest
in a saucepan until the butter melts.
Mix the egg yolks and 2 tablespoons
sugar together, and then blend in the
warm milk. Put the breadcrumbs into
the bottom of a buttered 1½-2 pint
ovenproof dish. Pour over the egg yolk
and milk mixture, and leave to stand
for 15 minutes. Bake in a moderate
oven for 25-30 minutes until the
custard is set.
Whisk the egg whites until stiff.
Whisk in half the remaining sugar,
and then fold in the final amount.
Spread the jam over the set custard
and spoon the meringue mixture on
top. Bake for 15-20 minutes until the
meringue is golden.
Serve hot or cold.

Crème Brûlée
Burnt cream

SERVES 4-6

Oven temperature:
Very cool 275°F (Gas Mark ½, 140°C)
Cooking time:
1 hour

4 egg yolks
4 tablespoons sugar
½ pint double [1¼ cups heavy] cream
½ pint single [1¼ cups light] cream
¼ teaspoon vanilla essence
castor [fine] sugar for topping
green grapes

Beat the egg yolks with the sugar
in a bowl, or the top of a double
saucepan. Heat all of the cream together
in a pan. Bring the creams just to
simmering point, then pour them over
the egg yolks and mix well. Put the top
of the double saucepan or the bowl over
a pan of gently simmering water and
cook, stirring constantly, until the
mixture coats the back of a wooden
spoon. Add the vanilla essence. Strain
the custard into a 1½-pint ovenproof
dish. Cover this with foil, and stand the
dish in a baking tin containing about
1-inch warm water. Bake the custard
for about 45 minutes, or until it is firm.
Remove it from the oven and allow
to cool, then chill for about 4 hours,
or preferably overnight. Sprinkle the
surface of the custard with sugar
so that it is completely covered. Put
under hot grill [broiler], heat slowly so
that the sugar melts and caramelises.
Remove from the heat, cool, and then
refrigerate for a further 3 hours.
Decorate with halved grapes before
serving.

Profiteroles

SERVES 6

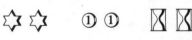

Oven temperature:
Fairly hot 400°F (Gas Mark 6, 200°C)
Cooking time:
About 25 minutes

2½ oz. choux pastry (see page 54)
5 fl. oz. double [heavy] cream
1 egg white
castor [fine] sugar
4 oz. plain [semi-sweet] chocolate
5 fl. oz. canned evaporated milk

Make up the choux pastry (see page 54).
Grease two baking trays. Using two
teaspoons to make a scoop, put
teaspoonfuls of the mixture on to the
baking trays, about 20 in all, spacing
evenly. Bake in a fairly hot oven for
about 25 minutes or until the buns are
well risen and golden. Remove from
the oven and allow to cool.
Lightly whip the cream. Stiffly whisk
the egg white and fold it into the cream.
Sweeten to taste. Split all the buns,
and fill with the cream. Pile them on to
a dish and chill.
Break the chocolate up into pieces
and put into a saucepan with the
evaporated milk. Put over a very gentle
heat until the chocolate has melted,
stirring from time to time. Allow the
sauce to cool. Then, just before
serving, thoroughly beat the sauce
and pour it over the choux buns.

Variation:
A small family block of ice cream
could be used in place of the fresh
cream. Put into the choux buns just
before serving. If you wanted to serve
only 4, you could make éclairs with
some of the choux pastry. Fill them
with the cream and ice with chocolate
glacé icing or with melted chocolate.

USEFUL RECIPES

Short crust pastry

8 oz. [2 cups] **plain flour**
pinch salt
4 oz. [½ cup] **fat, butter, margarine,**
  or a mixture of margarine and lard
about 4 tablespoons cold water

Sieve together the flour and salt.
Cut the fat into small pieces and,
using your fingertips, rub it into the
flour until the mixture resembles fine
breadcrumbs. Add the water, using a
palette knife to cut and stir the mixture
thoroughly, so that it clings together
leaving the sides of the bowl clean.
Put the pastry on to a floured board
or working surface, and knead *very
lightly* so that you have a smooth,
round ball. Roll out, and use as
required.
It is very important when making
short crust pastry to ensure that the
mixture is not overhandled, and that
you do not add too much water as
this makes the pastry tough, and causes
it to shrink considerably during the
cooking.
When a recipe calls for 6 ounces of
pastry, it is referring to pastry made
with 6 ounces [1½ cups] of flour.

To make a flan case

Place the flan ring on an upturned
baking tray, or use a sandwich tin.
For a 6-inch flan you need 4 ounces of
pastry, for a 7-9-inch flan you need
6 ounces of pastry and for a 10-12-inch
flan you need 8 ounces of pastry.
Roll the pastry out evenly into as neat
a circle as possible, about 2-inches
larger than the diameter of the flan
ring. Using the rolling pin for support,
carefully lift the pastry into the flan
ring. Then, with your index finger,
press the pastry down into the flan
ring and, if using a fluted flan ring, into
the flutes.

To neaten the edge of the flan, start
from the centre, and roll away from
you in a short stroke across the top of
the flan edge, so that excess pastry is
cut off around the top. Turn the flan
round and repeat the process. Now
either fill the flan and bake, or bake
blind.

To bake a flan case blind

Oven temperature:
Fairly hot 400°F (Gas Mark 6, 200°C)
Cooking time:
20 minutes

Put a sheet of greaseproof paper or
foil, about 4-inches larger than the
diameter of the flan, into the bottom of
the flan case, fitting it gently to the
shape. Fill with dry crusts of bread
or baking beans.
Put into a fairly hot oven, and bake for
10-15 minutes, or until the pastry is
set firm. Remove the greaseproof paper
and beans, and bake for a further
5-10 minutes to dry out the base.
The baking beans should be allowed
to cool, then put into a suitable
container. They can then be used
again.

Note: If you are using a china flan dish
you will probably find that the flan
case takes slightly longer to cook and
that fillings (such as the Cheese and
Spinach Flan on page 21) also take
longer to set. This is because the china
does not transmit the heat as fast as
metal.

Suet crust pastry

8 oz. [2 cups] **self-raising flour**
  (or plain flour with 2 teaspoons
  baking powder)
½ **teaspoon salt**
4 oz. [½ cup] **shredded beef suet**
about 5 fl. oz. water

Sieve together the flour, the baking
powder, if used, and the salt. Add the
suet, and mix with water until the
mixture binds together and leaves the
sides of the bowl clean.
Use in recipes as directed.
When a recipe calls for 8 ounces of
pastry, it is referring to pastry made
with 8 ounces [2 cups] of flour.

To cover a basin for steaming

Take two pieces of greased greaseproof
paper, or one piece of greased foil,
at least 6-inches wider than the
diameter of the top of the basin.
Make a pleat in the centre of this,
about 1-inch wide, to allow for the
pudding to expand. If using greaseproof
paper, put it over the top of the pudding
basin, pull taut, and tie in place with
string.
If using foil, you can either tie it into
place as above, or turn the edges of the
foil firmly under on itself, so that a
taut covering is formed.

Choux pastry

2½ oz. [⅝ cup] **plain flour**
pinch salt
4 **tablespoons butter or margarine**
5 **fl. oz. water**
1 **teaspoon sugar**
2 **eggs**
1 **egg yolk**

Sift the flour and salt together. Put
the butter or margarine, cut into small
pieces, into a pan with the water and
sugar. Bring slowly to the boil. Add the
flour, all at once, while the pan is still
on a low heat. Beat well until the
mixture forms a soft ball that leaves
the sides of the pan clean.
Remove from the heat, allow to cool
slightly, then beat in the eggs and egg
yolk one at a time until a very smooth,
shiny mixture results. Use as directed
in the recipe.

When a recipe calls for $2\frac{1}{2}$ ounces of choux pastry it is referring to pastry made with $2\frac{1}{2}$ ounces [$\frac{5}{8}$ cup] of flour.

Meringues

The method for making meringues is the same whether the mixture is to be dried out slowly in the oven, or to be served hot or cold on top of a pudding—as in the Queen of Puddings on page 52. If the mixture is to be used for a pudding, it uses less sugar.

2 egg whites
4 oz. castor or sieved icing [$\frac{1}{2}$ cup fine or 1 cup sifted confectioners'] sugar

Whisk the egg whites, which for the best results should be at room temperature, in a clean bowl until they are very stiff. You should be able to turn the bowl upside down without any of the mixture falling out. *Gradually* beat in half of the sugar, a teaspoon at a time. Fold in the remaining sugar. If you are using an electric mixer it is possible to beat in the remainder of the sugar gradually. This will result in a very stiff meringue which is good for piping.
Either pile the mixture on top of a pudding or flan and bake as directed, or put spoonfuls (or pipe rosettes) on to baking trays lined with greased greaseproof paper or special non-stick baking paper. Bake in a very cool oven, 250°F (Gas Mark $\frac{1}{4}$, 130°C) for about 2 hours or until the meringues have dried out.
Serve on their own with cold desserts or sandwich together with cream.

Coating food with egg and breadcrumbs before frying

The easiest way to do this is to set up a 'production line'. On the one side you need a board or plate, for the food to be coated. Next to that put a flat plate for flour, seasoned with salt and pepper.
Beat an egg with 1 tablespoon water, strain it on to another flat plate, and place it next to the seasoned flour. Straining the egg is important, as otherwise you will find that you have 'strands' of egg which give an uneven coating.
Put some breadcrumbs (use either dried crumbs or fresh white crumbs) on a third plate and place this next to the egg. Finally put another plate or board at the end of the line for the coated food.
First lightly toss the food in the seasoned flour; this helps the egg to adhere to the food. Next dip it in the egg, then lift it out and allow any excess to drip back into the plate. Then dip in the breadcrumbs, and turn until evenly coated. Finally put on to the board or plate ready for frying. If you have time, it is best to refrigerate the food for about an hour before frying, as this gives the coating a chance to become firm and set.

Note: For small pieces of food, you may find it easier to have the flour and breadcrumbs in plastic or brown paper bags. Drop the pieces of food in, and shake gently until they are thoroughly coated.

To make stock

Stock can be made from raw or cooked bones. It is particularly wasteful to throw away the bones of a chicken, turkey or duck, as these can very easily be used to make a nourishing soup. Put the bones (beef marrow bones make particularly good stock), into a large saucepan and cover them with cold salted water. Bring to the boil and skim. Cover, and cook very slowly for about 3 hours, topping up with a little extra water if necessary. Strain the stock from the bones, and skim again. Keep in the refrigerator until required, but boil up again every 2-3 days, to keep it wholesome. Vegetables may be added to the stock to give extra flavour, but in this case the stock does not keep as well. The best and most usual additions are carrot, onion, turnip, celery and mushroom stalks, and a bouquet garni of herbs may also be added.

Tomato sauce

Makes about $\frac{1}{2}$ pint [$1\frac{1}{4}$ cups]
Cooking time:
35 minutes

1 tablespoon butter or margarine
1 slice streaky bacon, de-rinded and chopped
1 small onion, finely chopped
8 oz. canned tomatoes
good pinch dried basil
salt and pepper

Melt the butter or margarine in a pan. Fry the bacon and onion in this for about 5 minutes, over a medium heat. Add the tomatoes and basil, and season with the salt and pepper. Cover and simmer for about 30 minutes.
If the sauce is too thin, cook it fast for a few minutes in an open pan, to reduce it. Serve with meat loaves, spaghetti or noodles.

White sauce

Coating consistency
Makes $\frac{1}{2}$ pint [$1\frac{1}{4}$ cups]
Cooking time:
About 8 minutes

2 tablespoons butter or margarine
4 tablespoons flour
$\frac{1}{2}$ pint [$1\frac{1}{4}$ cups] milk, or milk and fish or meat stock
salt and pepper

Melt the butter or margarine in a saucepan. Stir in the flour and cook for about a minute over a low heat. This mixture is known as a 'roux'. Remove it from the heat and gradually stir in the milk, or the milk and fish or meat stock mixture. Return to the heat and bring to the boil, stirring all the time.
Cook for about 3 minutes. Season to taste.

Note: For a thin white sauce, use only 1 tablespoon fat and 2 tablespoons flour to ½ pint [1¼ cups] milk. For a thick panada, used as a basis for soufflés and fish cakes, use 2 tablespoons fat and 8 tablespoons flour to ½ pint [1¼ cups] milk.

Béchamel sauce

generous ½ pint [1¼ cups] milk
1 bay leaf
3 peppercorns
1 blade mace
few parsley stalks
piece of carrot
½ onion
2 tablespoons butter
4 tablespoons flour
salt and pepper
Put the milk into a saucepan with the bay leaf, peppercorns, mace, parsley, carrot and onion. Bring slowly to the boil, cover, and simmer very gently for 10 minutes. Strain.
Melt the butter in a pan, add the flour, and then make up as for the White Sauce this page, using the strained flavoured milk.

French dressing

The ingredients for French Dressing and the proportion of vinegar to oil is very largely a matter of personal taste, but this is a good basic recipe which will give enough dressing to toss a salad for 4 people.

¼ teaspoon French mustard
pinch sugar
pinch salt
freshly milled black pepper
1 tablespoon vinegar
2 tablespoons oil

Either mix together the mustard, sugar, salt, pepper and vinegar in a basin, and then add in the oil, or put all the ingredients into a screw-topped jar and shake well. In either case, make sure all ingredients are thoroughly combined.
French dressing can be stored for months in a bottle in a cool place, and it is a good idea to make up a large quantity so that you always have some to hand.

Variations:
The above is a very simple dressing, and any of the following ingredients can also be added:
§ Chopped chives, parsley or basil.
§ A little very finely chopped onion.
§ A crushed clove of garlic.
§ A few very finely chopped capers.

Mayonnaise

Makes ½ pint [1¼ cups]

2 egg yolks
½ teaspoon dry mustard
½ teaspoon salt
pepper
2 tablespoons wine vinegar or
  lemon juice
½ pint [1¼ cups] oil

For the best results, have all the ingredients at room temperature. You can make mayonnaise from eggs straight from the refrigerator, but there will be a much greater chance of it curdling.
Beat the egg yolks with the mustard, salt, pepper and 1 tablespoon vinegar. Use either a balloon whisk or a wooden

spoon for this, whichever you find easier. Now gradually beat in the oil, literally drop by drop, until you have added about half of it and the mixture looks thick and shiny. At this stage the oil can be added a little more quickly. Add the remaining vinegar when all the oil has been incorporated. If by chance you have added the oil too quickly at the beginning and the mixture does curdle, beat a fresh egg yolk in another basin, and beat the curdled mixture into this, a teaspoonful at a time.

If you want to thin the mayonnaise down a little, you may either add lemon juice, a little single [light] cream, or 1-2 teaspoons hot water. The thick mayonnaise can be put into a screw-topped jar or other suitable container and kept in the refrigerator for about 2 weeks.

COOKING FOR TWO

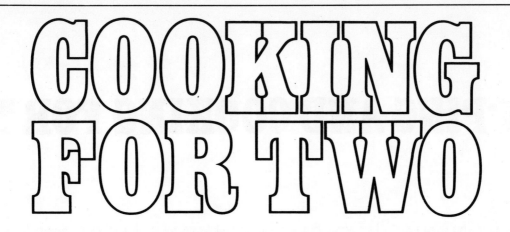

Most people have to cook for two sometimes—whether they're newly-weds, flat-sharing friends, parents of young children or a retired couple—and yet most recipes are geared to four, six or more servings and are often almost impossible to reduce. (How **can** you divide one egg white by three?) Here are recipes specifically designed for the person who is cooking for two, likes good food but resents the waste of over-buying. **All** the recipes in this section are for two and there are menus to suit all sorts of occasions. Here are delicious recipes for the shoe-string cook; a special occasion menu for when you want to splash out; we show you how to cook a whole meal in one pot; offer time-saving dishes to cook the day before; and cosy suppers on a tray. We suggest a variety of appetizers; special ways to cheer up vegetables; and a selection of mouth-watering fruits and desserts; we show you how to make a joint, turkey or duck economically and deliciously provide two or three different meals for two.

And, equally important, here too are lots of useful hints and ideas to help you organize your kitchen and budget for two with minimum wastage; what quantities to buy and how to plan your menus; how to store food and what equipment you will need.

SHOPPING AND COOKING FOR TWO

How many times have you tried to cook a meal for two, only to find that every recipe you read is intended for four, or even six, people? It is extremely frustrating to have to halve, quarter or even 'third' the ingredients listed, and of course, such things as '3 eggs' resolutely refuse to be divided! And yet, when you come to think of it, some of the most important meals in the world are just for two people: the relaxing dinner for mum and dad when the children have gone to bed; everyday meals for the older or retired couple; Sunday lunch for the newlyweds; or even that palpitating first (and *very* important) meal for the new boyfriend.

Recipes for all occasions

It is for these and many other occasions that *Cooking for Two* has been specially devised. Here are recipes for all contingencies, from the panic-stricken emergency to the long-planned special occasion. Here also are suggestions to make the routine everyday choices a bit more exciting and varied. If you envy the range of materials and scope of recipes available to large families or more ambitious hostesses, read on and discover that the more intimate meals you require need not be restricted or predictable.

Planning

There's no getting away from it. Before you can embark on a successful career of cooking for two, you must reconcile yourself to the fact that economical *and* imaginative meals call for a higher degree of organization in the kitchen. You need to know which items can profitably be bought in bulk, and which ones can't; which foods keep and for how long; how to create different dishes from the same basics; how to put the leftovers from one meal to good use in another. Native ingenuity will help you solve some of the problems as they come up, of

course. But you can in fact avoid most of them entirely by common sense. And that means planning your meals more than one day ahead—preferably for the whole week, if you have to go out to work during the day and your shopping time is limited.

An economic roasting joint

Take meat for example. Many families of two don't ever have a roast —simply because it is not worth buying a large and costly joint of good roasting meat just for two people. Or is it? Maybe we can learn something here from our ancestors whose vast joints served the entire family from Sunday to Friday inclusive, like the old recipe for Vicarage Mutton: hot on Sunday, cold on Monday, hashed on Tuesday, minced on Wednesday, curried on Thursday, and broth on Friday!
Even with modern refrigeration that's asking a bit much for two people. All the same, there are many splendid recipes that call for cooked meat—as you'll see from this book. So why not have a proper roast on Sunday and get at least two more imaginative meals from the same joint. This, of course, will justify the cost of the meat in the first place: in fact, it's just as economic as buying three separate smaller items.

Cooking ahead

Equally important for the busy cook are the advantages of cooking ahead. To prepare two or three casseroles or cook-ahead dishes at the same time actually takes little more time than preparing one. And, of course, some casseroles and curries improve with keeping for a day or so and then being re-heated. And at the same time rather than simply throwing away the bones of the joint or feeding them to a friendly dog, it calls for very little effort and even less time to put them into a stockpot with a few leftover (or fresh) vegetables and some seasoning

to make a fine rich stock. With the advent of instant stock cubes, this culinary art is dying out—sadly, because nothing can really replace a true homemade stock. But to deny yourselves this luxury because there are only two of you would be a total surrender to 'convenience' cooking.

Buying

Luckily canned foods, and to a large extent, packet foods, come in varying sizes. It would be foolish to buy a 15 ounce can of fruit, for example, when an 11 ounce one would be more sensible. There is nothing worse than having half a tin of peaches or tomatoes mouldering in valuable refrigerator space until it simply *has* to be thrown away. However, even for two, buying in bulk can save money with some items. Good olive oil works out much cheaper (about half price in some cases) if bought in half or one gallon cans. And if kept in a cool, dark place it will keep in indefinitely.
There are some things which self-evidently should *not* be bought in large quantities: eggs, coffee (which rapidly loses its fragrance even in bean form) and salad vegetables, about which more later. On the other hand, rice, cereals, flour, sugar and pasta are worthwhile bought in bulk, and should be stored in airtight tins or glass jars. And if you're cooking with wine— and propose to drink some with the meal as well—it makes more sense to buy one of the litre bottles which most shippers are putting on the market nowadays. Use it for both cooking and drinking. Very often the litre bottles come with plastic fitted caps and, once opened, will keep adequately for 2-3 days.

Storing

Naturally, in the end the quantities of food you can buy depend on how long they will keep and what storage facilities you have at your disposal. If you are the proud owner of a deep-freeze, you have few problems. However, a large freezing compartment in the refrigerator is quite suitable for two—but do take proper notice of the maker's recommended storage times for frozen foods.

With fresh foods, there are very few that come naturally in quantities which relate to two people. One lettuce, for example, might be too much for two on one day; therefore it needs to be stored in an airtight plastic container in the bottom of the refrigerator. (This is where your shopping must be geared to your planning—you should really plan for salad on consecutive days, not a week ahead, though obviously there's no need to settle for the same kind of salad two days running.) To help you avoid overstocking—which may well be your biggest single source of waste—here is a list of the average storage times of major items.

Meat

All meat should be put into the refrigerator, after being wiped and wrapped in foil, immediately after you get home from shopping. Joints will keep up to 5 days, steaks and chops rather less, bacon slightly longer. Cooked meat will also keep from 3-5 days if kept in an airtight container.

Fish

Fish should be eaten as fresh as possible, and whether cooked or uncooked, within 2 days at the most. For frozen fish, consult the star ratings on the refrigerator, and keep in the freezing compartment.

Poultry

Fresh poultry, drawn and wrapped in foil will keep up to three days, as will cooked birds if placed in the refrigerator as soon as they have cooled. Frozen ducks, chicken etc. should be kept wrapped, in the freezer, or for not more than 2 days in the main body of the refrigerator.

Vegetables

Salad vegetables such as lettuce will keep up to 4 or 5 days in an airtight container in the bottom of the refrigerator. Greens will stay fresh for up to a week in the vegetable compartment. For frozen vegetables, follow the manufacturer's instructions.

Cheese

Hard cheeses are best stored in the main body of the refrigerator, wrapped in foil, but they should be taken out a couple of hours before use. Soft cheeses should only be bought as and when required.

Eggs

Eggs should not be kept in the refrigerator. Keep them in a cool dark cupboard for up to a fortnight, if they were fresh when bought. Whole yolks can be covered with water and will keep adequately for 2 or 3 days, and egg whites will last up to 4 days in an airtight container.

Herbs and spices

It is of course, impossible and unnecessary to buy spices in very minute quantities. A basic spice rack of ground spices (cinnamon, cloves, coriander, cumin, paprika, turmeric etc.) is a good investment, however many people you have to cook for. But certain spices, like nutmeg, are best bought whole and grated as required—and that applies especially to pepper which rapidly loses its fragrance and aroma unless bought as whole peppercorns and ground from a pepper mill.

In season, it is a good idea to have your own fresh herbs growing in the kitchen or in a window box. Mint, parsley and chives are particularly useful and their growth will just keep pace with the requirements of cooking for two.

Equipment

Finally a word about kitchen equipment, which is so much more important than many people think. In order to cook well you must have the basic tools available, otherwise everything will be twice as hard and take up so much more precious time. First and foremost, every cook needs a good set of knives—the carbonated steel ones are the best and sharpest—and to begin with you should have at least three of varying length. To keep them sharp, use an ordinary butcher's steel or sharpening stone. Next on the list is a palette knife, a fish slice, a long-handled spoon for basting, a perforated draining spoon, and of course a set of wooden spoons. For whisking egg whites, nothing does the job better than a balloon whisk, and for other whisking chores a rotary whisk or an electric hand whisk are ideal. A chopping board is important because if you chop things on other surfaces you ruin both your knives and the surfaces. Every kitchen should have a lemon squeezer, a four-sided grater, a sieve and a colander for draining vegetables. Other items of great priority are weighing scales and a measuring jug (or a set of measuring cups for American households)—trying to guess what 3 ounces looks like is sheer misery when you're in a hurry. Obviously you need the usual complement of saucepans (with well-fitting lids), meat tins and baking tins, plus a small oven-proof *gratin* dish and a casserole. But if you're fortunate to have collected all these things already—then the one luxury item on this list of essentials has to be a blender—invaluable for puréeing and making soups.

BREAKFAST

Breakfast can be one of the most pleasant meals to share, and it seems a pity not to get up just a little earlier to enjoy the pleasures of a leisurely breakfast together.

Bacon and Mushroom Scramble

☆ ① ✕

Preparation and cooking time:
15 minutes
This is a basic scramble recipe. Bacon and mushroom is a traditional combination, but you can vary it according to what is available— tomatoes, chopped peppers, onion, kidney, flaked smoked haddock or chicken livers can make a nice change.

3 bacon slices
1½ oz. [3 tablespoons] butter
1 teaspoon cooking oil
2 oz. mushrooms
2 eggs
salt
freshly ground black pepper

Fry the bacon in 1 ounce of butter and the oil until crisp. Remove from the pan, chop into small pieces and keep warm.
Slice the mushrooms and fry them for a few minutes, then transfer them to the bacon dish.
Melt the remaining butter in a thick bottomed saucepan without browning. Whisk the eggs in a bowl and pour them in to the saucepan. Stir continuously with a wooden spoon over medium heat, allowing the eggs to cook without sticking to the bottom or sides of the pan.

Opposite: Country breakfast with Homemade Muesli and Toasted Oatcakes with Bacon and Apple

When the egg is three-quarters cooked, remove the pan from the heat, add the fat from the frying pan and continue stirring away from the heat until all liquid is absorbed and the eggs are soft and glossy. Then fold in the bacon and mushrooms, season to taste with salt and pepper, and serve immediately on hot buttered toast.

Toasted Oatcakes with Bacon and Apple

☆ ① ✕

Preparation and cooking time:
30 minutes
Oatcakes have been eaten in Britain for centuries. Here is a savoury version with bacon and apple topping but they are delicious served with grilled [broiled] tomatoes and sausages, or spread with creamy butter and marmalade or homemade preserves.

3 oz. [¾ cup] medium-ground oatmeal
1 oz. wholemeal [4 tablespoons wholewheat] flour
¼ teaspoon salt
1½ tablespoons butter
1 tablespoon boiling water
4 bacon slices, crisply fried
4 apple rings, fried

Heat the oven to 350°F (Gas Mark 4 180°C).
Put the oatmeal, flour and salt in a mixing bowl and rub together thoroughly. Melt the butter in a small pan over low heat without browning.
Make a well in the centre of the oatmeal mixture, pour the melted butter into it and start to mix in with a fork. Add a tablespoon of boiling water and continue mixing to dough consistency with lightly floured hands.
Sprinkle a little flour and oatmeal

on to a pastry-board. Roll out the dough to ¼-inch thickness and cut into rounds with a 2½ inch diameter pastry cutter. Lift the oatcakes on to a lightly-greased baking-sheet and bake on the top shelf of the oven for 20 minutes.
Serve the cooked oatcakes topped with crisp bacon, fried apple rings and mustard or a sharp pickle.

Homemade Muesli

☆ ① ✕ ✕

Preparation time:
15 minutes—plus 8 hours
Many shops now sell various brands of ready made muesli, but it really is a lot nicer when prepared at home, using fresh ingredients. This version—with dried apricots—can be made all the year round but, of course, you can vary the fruits according to season and availability. And you can experiment with different nuts, as well.

2 tablespoons medium-ground oatmeal
2 oz. [⅓ cup] dried apricots
1 red dessert apple
the juice of half a lemon
4 tablespoons soft brown sugar
1 teaspoon ground cinnamon
4 oz. [1 cup] chopped walnuts
5 fl. oz. [⅝ cup] natural yogurt

Soak the oatmeal overnight in 5 fluid ounces [⅝ cup] of water. Put the apricots in a separate bowl, cover with water and also leave to soak overnight.
Next morning drain the apricots, pat them dry with absorbent kitchen paper chop roughly and add them to the soaked oatmeal.
Core and roughly chop the apple (leaving on the skins,) and toss in lemon juice. Stir in to the oatmeal and apricot mixture. Sprinkle on first the brown sugar, then the cinnamon and finally the coarsely chopped walnuts.
Serve with fresh yogurt.

LIGHT LUNCHES

Here are recipes specifically designed for those who plan to eat their main meal in the evening, and want something nutritious but simple at midday. The dishes can be eaten at home, of course, or made up into lunch boxes to eat on a journey or, for the working couple, they make an appetizing alternative to café sandwiches or canteen food. Simply wrap the food in aluminium foil, add a paper napkin and a piece of fruit or some salad vegetables, and you have a perfectly balanced packed meal. It can be unwrapped without fuss in a car or train, carried into the park for a fresh air lunch break, or eaten in the office if the weather turns nasty.

Tortilla

☆　　①　　◻

Preparation and cooking time:
20 minutes
This is a huge, flat Spanish-style omelette—a meal on its own. A single one is enough for two people and the fillings can be varied. The version given here is sometimes called a tortilla Castellana.

2 teaspoons olive oil
1 tablespoon butter
1 large onion, chopped
4 medium-sized potatoes, cooked
　and diced
1 tablespoon freshly chopped parsley
4 large eggs, lightly beaten
salt
freshly ground black pepper

Melt the oil and butter in an 8-inch frying pan. Fry the onion gently for 10 minutes, or until almost cooked. Add the diced potato and heat through stirring now and then. Then add the parsley.
Season the eggs with salt and freshly

ground black pepper to taste. Turn the heat up high, pour the egg mixture into the pan and quickly reduce the heat to moderate. Run a palette knife round the edge and shake the pan to avoid sticking. Lift the omelette slightly with the palette knife and, when cooked and golden underneath, slide it out onto a warm plate then return to the pan to cook the reverse side. Serve cold.

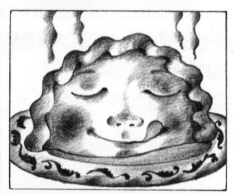

Homemade Cornish Pasties

☆　　①　①　　◻　◻

Preparation and cooking time: *1¼ hours*
This homemade version of the famous English classic is a pleasant treat and equally good hot or cold.

8 oz. sirloin steak
1 medium-sized onion, chopped
1 medium-sized potato, diced
salt
freshly ground black pepper
1½ teaspoons dried mixed herbs
8 oz. shortcrust pastry
1 egg, beaten

Heat the oven to 425°F (Gas Mark 7, 220°C).
Cut the steak into very small pieces and mix in the onion and potato. Season with salt, freshly ground black pepper and mixed herbs.
Divide the pastry into 2 and on a floured board roll out each piece into an 8-inch round. Place half the meat mixture into the centre of each pastry round. Dampen the edges of the pastry with a little water and

draw them together in the centre, sealing well. Flute the edges and brush all over with the beaten egg.
Place the pasties on a baking tray and bake for 15 minutes, then reduce heat to 350°F (Gas Mark 4, 180°C) and cook for a further 40 minutes.

Meat Loaf

☆　　①　　◻　◻

Preparation and cooking time:
1½ hours
This meat loaf can be served hot with homemade tomato sauce (basic recipe) for a light lunch, or it is just as good served cold cut into thick slices for a packed lunch-box. It could even be sliced and put into sandwiches. This recipe will provide enough for two meals.

1 lb. lean minced [ground] beef
8 oz. pork sausage meat
2 large onions, minced
1 garlic clove, crushed
1 teaspoon dried mixed herbs
salt
freshly ground black pepper
2 slices bread
2 tablespoons milk
1 egg, beaten

Heat the oven to 375°F (Gas Mark 5, 190°C).
Put the minced [ground] beef into a large mixing-bowl. Add the sausage meat, minced onions, garlic, herbs and a good seasoning of salt and freshly ground black pepper.
Remove the crust from the bread and soak the slices in the milk. Squeezing out the excess milk, add the bread to the rest of the ingredients, and mix everything together as thoroughly and evenly as possible. Then add the beaten egg and bind the mixture together.
Press the mixture into a 2 pound loaf tin and bake for 1¼ hours.

Opposite: Take Homemade Cornish Pasties and Meat Loaf for a packed lunch. Inset: Tortilla

INSTANT DINNERS

Florentine Plaice (Flounder) Fillets

☆　　①　　▨

Preparation and cooking time:
25 minutes
Here is an instant freezer meal,
but do remember to remove the
packages from the freezer in good
time, so that they are thoroughly
defrosted before you start cooking.

6 oz. frozen chopped spinach
salt
freshly ground black pepper
8 oz. frozen plaice [flounder] fillets
5 fl. oz. [⅝ cup] instant cheese sauce
　(from a packet or basic recipe)
freshly grated nutmeg
1 tablespoon double [heavy]
　cream
1½ oz. [⅓ cup] Cheddar cheese,
　grated
1 tablespoon breadcrumbs
1 tablespoon butter

Heat the oven to 350°F (Gas Mark 4,
180°C).
Butter a shallow baking dish and place
the spinach in it. Season with salt
and freshly ground black pepper.
Arrange the fish fillets on top of the
spinach and season again.
Make up the cheese sauce according to
the instructions on the packet and
add a few good gratings of nutmeg.
Pour the sauce over the fish and
sprinkle the grated cheese and
breadcrumbs on top.
Dot with flecks of butter and bake on
the top shelf of the oven for 20
minutes.

Instant Chilli con Carne

☆　　①　　▨

Preparation and cooking time:
15-20 minutes
This one really is absolutely instant
but, on days when you have a little
more time to spare, you can make it
even nicer by using freshly cooked
minced [ground] beef.

1 oz. [2 tablespoons] butter
1 medium-sized onion, chopped
1 small red pepper, chopped
15 oz. canned savoury minced steak
15 oz. canned red kidney beans
1 tablespoon tomato purée
2 teaspoons chilli con carne
　seasoning (or powdered chilli)
salt
freshly ground black pepper

Melt the butter and fry the chopped
onion and pepper in it until soft
(about 10-15 minutes).
Add the minced [ground] steak, the
drained kidney beans, tomato purée
and chilli powder. Season with salt
and pepper. Stir thoroughly and heat
through.
Serve with crusty bread and butter,
and a side salad.

Chicken Veronique

☆　　①①　　▨

Preparation and cooking time:
30 minutes
Here is a very handy recipe for
jazzing-up shop bought, pre-cooked
chicken pieces. When you get the
chicken home, remove all the skin,
discard it, then separate the flesh
from the bones.

10½ fl. oz. [1¼ cups] canned
　condensed chicken soup
2½ fl. oz. [¼ cup] dry white wine
2 large cooked chicken breasts
salt
freshly ground black pepper
2 tablespoons double [heavy]
　cream
4 oz. white grapes, halved and
　seeded

In a large saucepan bring the
condensed soup and white wine to
simmering point. Strain the liquid into
a clean saucepan, add the chicken and
simmer very gently for 20-25
minutes until the chicken is
thoroughly heated through.
Meanwhile, heat the grill [broiler].
Remove the saucepan from the heat,
season, stir in the cream and grapes
and pour the mixture into an
ovenproof serving dish. Cook under
the hot grill [broiler] until the sauce
begins to bubble.
Serve with tinned new potatoes and a
side salad.

*Opposite: When you're in a hurry,
try Chicken Veronique, with grapes,
wine and a quick, creamy sauce.*

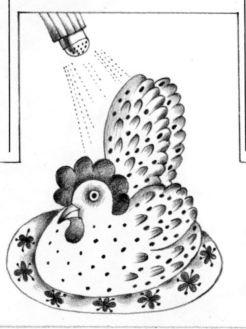

ONE-POT CASSEROLES

Casseroling is a miraculous way of cooking: cheap, tough cuts of meat are transformed into mouth-watering gourmet treats. Slow, moist cooking tenderizes the meat (and all the nutrients are captured in the gravy) but, although cooking time is lengthy, not much work is required of the cook.

Traditional Irish Stew with Parsley Dumplings *(see left)*

☆ ① ⊠ ⊠ ⊠

Preparation and cooking time: $2\frac{3}{4}$ hours
On a cold and frosty day it is hard to beat an Irish Stew. It's so easy to prepare and very warming—all you need is a large cooking pot and some big soup-plates to serve it in.

2 lb. middle neck and scrag end of lamb, mixed
2 tablespoons flour, seasoned with salt and pepper
2 large onions, sliced
8 oz. potatoes, cut into chunks
1 tablespoon pearl barley
$\frac{1}{2}$ teaspoon mixed herbs
15 fl. oz. [2 cups] boiling water
For the parsley dumplings:
2 oz. [$\frac{1}{4}$ cup] shredded suet
4 oz. [1 cup] self-raising flour
1 tablespoon freshly chopped parsley
salt
freshly ground black pepper

Toss the pieces of lamb in the seasoned flour, then put them into a saucepan together with the sliced onion, potatoes and pearl barley. Sprinkle on the mixed herbs and another good seasoning of salt and freshly ground black pepper.
Pour on the boiling water and bring to the boil. Remove any scum that may have formed on top. Reduce the heat, cover the saucepan with a lid and simmer very gently for $2\frac{1}{2}$ hours.
To make the dumplings, mix the suet, flour and parsley together, add pepper and salt and enough water to make a fairly elastic dough. Divide the dough into 4, and roll each piece into a round.
20-25 minutes before the end of cooking time check that the stew is on the boil, and drop the dumplings into the pan. Replace the lid and finish cooking at boiling point.
Serve immediately with buttered carrots if extra vegetables are required.

Simple Strogonoff

☆ ① ① ⊠ ⊠

Preparation and cooking time:
2-$2\frac{1}{4}$ hours
The classic version of Filet de Boeuf Strogonoff is made with tiny strips of fillet steak, sautéed and served in sour cream sauce. This variation, although made with a cheaper cut of meat, is just as exciting.

1 lb. lean chuck steak
1 tablespoon seasoned flour
a little dripping or cooking oil
1 medium-sized onion, chopped
1 teaspoon tomato purée
5 fl. oz. [$\frac{5}{8}$ cup] canned condensed mushroom soup
$2\frac{1}{2}$ fl. oz. [$\frac{1}{4}$ cup] natural yogurt
salt
freshly ground black pepper

Heat oven to 300°F (Gas Mark 1-2, 150°C).
Cut the meat into bite-sized chunks and toss in the seasoned flour.
Heat some dripping (or cooking oil) in a thick-bottomed saucepan, and fry the meat to brown nicely. Add the onion and continue to cook for 1-2 minutes. Then stir in the tomato purée, add the soup and yogurt and season with a little more pepper and salt.
Stir thoroughly, place the lid on the saucepan and simmer very gently on top of the stove—or in a low oven—for $1\frac{1}{2}$-2 hours, or until the meat is tender.

Veal Marengo

☆ ① ① ⊠ ⊠

Preparation and cooking time:
$1\frac{1}{4}$ hours
Being left with only one saucepan after a battle, Napoleon's chef improvised this garnish—originally for chicken, but it goes just as well with veal. There is no need for this dish to be expensive if you ask your butcher to sell you cut-up pie or stewing veal.

1 oz. [2 tablespoons] butter
1 large onion, sliced
1 lb. lean veal, cut into cubes
1 small green pepper, chopped
$1\frac{1}{2}$ teaspoons flour
$\frac{1}{2}$ teaspoon of dried mixed herbs
1 garlic clove, crushed
2 tablespoons tomato purée
5 fl. oz. [$\frac{5}{8}$ cup] dry white wine
$2\frac{1}{2}$ fl. oz. [$\frac{1}{4}$ cup] good stock (basic recipe)
salt
freshly ground black pepper

Heat the oven to 350°F (Gas Mark 4, 180°C).
Melt the butter in a thick-bottomed pan and gently fry the onion until it has turned pale gold. Then add the veal and brown very lightly. Next add the chopped pepper and allow that to fry for 1-2 minutes.
Stir in the flour, followed by the herbs and garlic. Add the tomato purée, and finally the wine and stock.
Stir well. Season to taste with salt and freshly ground black pepper. Place the lid on the casserole and cook in the oven for 1 hour.

DEAD-BROKE DINNERS

This is the section to read, and here are the recipes to follow when your funds are very low, or when you want to cut down on housekeeping expenses because you're saving up for something special like a holiday.

Contrary to popular belief, there is no reason why lack of money has to restrict you to a mundane diet, or prevents you from eating very tasty and nutritious foods. Even meat like lamb need not be beyond your budget. Select a cheap cut and carefully cook it with aromatic herbs to make it really inviting. Enjoy the challenge, experiment with foods and cooking methods that may be new to you, and see just what delicious dishes you can conjure from a shoestring budget.

Ragout of Mutton

Preparation and cooking time:
2¼ hours

2 lb. scrag end or middle neck of mutton or lamb
salt and freshly ground black pepper
1 tablespoon mutton dripping
2 medium-sized onions, roughly chopped
1 garlic clove, chopped
1 teaspoon mixed herbs
1 bay leaf
1 tablespoon flour
10 fl. oz. [1¼ cups] boiling water
6 small new potatoes, scrubbed
2 medium-sized tomatoes

Heat the oven to 315°F (Gas Mark 3½, 157°C).
Season the pieces of meat with salt and freshly ground pepper, then fry them in the dripping. When browned turn the meat into a casserole.
Fry the onions and garlic for a few minutes, then add them to the meat and sprinkle on the mixed herbs.
To the remaining juices in the pan add the flour and stir over low heat until smooth. Then add the boiling water, in a slow trickle, stirring all the time until you have a smooth gravy. When it reaches boiling-point pour the gravy over the meat.
Cover the casserole with a well fitting lid and cook in the oven for 1 hour. Then add the potatoes and tomatoes and cook for a further hour.
Taste to check the seasoning and serve with a green vegetable.

Curried Eggs

Preparation and cooking time:
50 minutes

2 oz. [4 tablespoons] butter
1 small onion, chopped
1 small cooking apple, peeled and chopped
2 teaspoons curry powder
¼ teaspoon ground turmeric
¼ teaspoon ground ginger
1½ oz. [6 tablespoons] flour
2 teaspoons lemon juice
10 fl. oz. [1¼ cups] chicken stock (basic recipe)
salt and freshly ground black pepper
4 eggs
4 oz. [1¾ cups] plain boiled or pilau rice (basic recipe)

Melt the butter in a heavy pan over low heat and gently fry the onion for about 10 minutes, until it has turned golden brown. Then add the apple, curry powder, the spices and flour, and stir to blend evenly. Pour on the lemon juice and then the stock very gradually, stirring all the time to prevent lumps from forming.
Bring the sauce to simmering point. Season with salt and freshly ground black pepper and simmer very gently for 30 minutes, covered.
Meanwhile put the eggs into a saucepan of cold water, bring to the boil, then simmer for exactly 7 minutes. Peel the shells from the cooked eggs, cut them into quarters and place in a warm serving dish.
Pour the curry sauce over the eggs. Serve with pilau rice and mango chutney.

Braised Pork with Apples

Preparation and cooking time:
1 hour 20 minutes

1 lb. lean belly pork strips
a little lard or dripping
salt and freshly ground black pepper
1 teaspoon dried sage
1 large onion, sliced
1 large cooking apple, peeled, cored and chopped
2 tablespoons water
12 oz. potatoes
a little butter

Heat the oven to 375°F (Gas Mark 5, 190°C).
Trim off a little of the surplus fat from the edge of the pork strips, then fry them in lard or dripping to brown on both sides.
Lay the pork strips on the bottom of a casserole and season with salt and freshly ground black pepper. Sprinkle on the dried sage.
Fry the onion to a pale golden colour then arrange over the pork together with the chopped apple. Season with a little more salt and pepper, and pour on the water.
Peel and slice the potatoes thinly and arrange them on top of the casserole —overlapping like slates on a roof. Season with more pepper and salt, dot with a few flecks of butter and bake, uncovered, for 1 hour. Serve with a green vegetable.

Opposite: Braised Pork with Apples. Inset: Curried Eggs

SUPPERS ON A TRAY

Here are recipes for when you want a quick delicious bite to eat before going out; for when you feel lazy and don't want to spend much time cooking; or for when you want to enjoy a cosy, casual meal. What could be nicer or more relaxed than supper on a tray! Make long, cold drinks and carry the tray into the garden on an evening when the weather is fine, or curl up by the fireside on a cold Winter's night, to watch television, listen to records, play chess or simply talk.

Spaghetti alla Carbonara

☆　　①　　☒

Preparation and cooking time:
15-20 minutes

8 oz. spaghetti
salt
1½ oz. [3 tablespoons] butter
2 teaspoons oil
half a medium-sized onion, finely
　chopped
4 oz. lean bacon, cut into strips
2 egg yolks
2½ fl. oz. single [¼ cup light] cream
8 tablespoons finely grated
　Parmesan
freshly ground black pepper

Cook the spaghetti in a large saucepan of salted boiling water until 'al dente' —about 11 minutes.
Meanwhile heat the butter and oil together in a saucepan and sauté the onion in it until soft but not brown. Then add the bacon strips and cook for a further 5 minutes.
Blend the egg yolks together with the cream and 6 tablespoons of grated Parmesan.
When the spaghetti is cooked, drain in a colander and return it to a dry hot pan. Pour the bacon and onion mixture over the spaghetti, followed by the egg and cream. Toss thoroughly and season with salt and pepper.
Serve immediately with the remaining Parmesan cheese sprinkled over.

Chef's Salad

☆　　①　①　　☒

Preparation time:
10 minutes
This is basically a cold meat salad. It can be adapted for any cold meats that are available, and whatever salad vegetables are in season at the time.

4 oz. cold roast beef
4 oz. cooked ham
4 oz. Swiss cheese
1 small lettuce heart
1 hardboiled egg, cut in half
2 tomatoes, quartered
2 celery stalks, finely chopped
1 small onion, finely chopped
4 sprigs of watercress

Cut the beef and ham into thin strips, also the cheese.
Divide the lettuce leaves between them on 2 plates. Arrange the strips of beef, ham and cheese on the lettuce leaves and place the hardboiled egg and tomato around them.
Sprinkle the chopped onion and celery all over and garnish with sprigs of watercress.
Serve with crusty fresh bread and a well flavoured vinaigrette dressing.

Salmon Loaf

☆　　①　　☒　☒　☒

Preparation time:
10 minutes plus 4 hours
This is a perfect dish for a summer evening, even if fresh salmon is beyond your budget. It should be served with a cucumber salad and some crusty fresh bread and butter.

7½ oz. canned salmon
2 oz. [4 tablespoons] butter, at room
　temperature
1 tablespoon mayonnaise
1 small onion, grated
1 celery stalk, finely chopped
1 tablespoon freshly chopped parsley
a pinch of salt
a pinch of cayenne pepper
4 sprigs watercress
1 hard-boiled egg

Turn the salmon out into a mixing bowl and mash to a pulp with a fork. Add the butter and mayonnaise and mix thoroughly until it becomes a smooth paste. Add the grated onion, celery, parsley, salt and cayenne pepper and mix thoroughly together.
Press the mixture into a small loaf tin or mould, cover lightly with aluminium foil and chill in the refrigerator for 4 hours.
To serve turn the salmon loaf out onto a serving dish and decorate with watercress and the hardboiled egg cut into slices.

Opposite: Spaghetti Alla Carbonara with a crisp, green salad

COOK AHEAD DISHES

Spiced Chicken

☆ ① ☒ ☒ ☒

Preparation and cooking time:
1 hour plus 4 hours
This recipe is not quite a curry, but is
mildly spiced. Its distinctive taste is a
delicious way to flavour ordinary
supermarket chicken.

2 chicken breasts
1 garlic clove, crushed
salt and freshly ground black pepper
1 teaspoon ground turmeric
1 teaspoon ground ginger
1 teaspoon curry powder
a little olive oil
1 oz. [2 tablespoons] butter
1 large onion, chopped
2 tablespoons natural yogurt
2 tablespoons single [light] cream

Place the chicken breasts in a small
roasting tin or oven-proof dish.
Prick the flesh all over with a skewer
and rub in the crushed garlic. Season
with salt and pepper.
Mix the spices together, then sprinkle
a third of the mixture over the
chicken. Pour a little olive oil over
and using your hands rub the spices
well into the meat. Cover the dish with
aluminium foil and leave in a cool
place for 3-4 hours.
Heat the oven to 350°F (Gas Mark 4,
180°C).
Spread the butter on to the chicken,
re-cover the dish with foil and bake
in the oven for 30 minutes.
Meanwhile gently fry the onion in a
little olive oil for about 10 minutes
or until soft. Then stir in the
remainder of the spice mixture, the
yogurt and cream.
Remove the chicken from the oven,
pour the spiced onion and yogurt
mixture over it, re-cover and bake for
a further 30 minutes.
10 minutes before the end of cooking
time remove the foil and baste
the chicken with the sauce.
If you are cooking only a little ahead
of the meal time, the dish can simply
remain in the oven—at low heat—for

an extra hour or so without coming to
any harm.
To reheat next day, put the covered
chicken dish in the oven (pre-heated
to the temperature stated above) for
20-25 minutes.

Cannelloni

☆ ① ☒ ☒

Preparation and cooking time:
1 hour 20 minutes

pancake batter (basic recipe)
10 fl. oz. [1¼ cups] cheese sauce
  (basic recipe)
freshly grated nutmeg
1 tablespoon grated Parmesan
For the filling:
1 onion, finely chopped
1 garlic clove, crushed
2 tablespoons oil
8 oz. minced [ground] beef
¼ teaspoon dried thyme
1 teaspoon dried basil
2 teaspoons tomato purée
8 oz. canned tomatoes
salt and freshly ground black pepper

First make the filling: in a saucepan
gently fry the onions and garlic in
the oil for about 10 minutes, then
add the minced [ground] beef and
brown it, carefully stirring all the
time to keep it separate.
Add the thyme, basil, tomato purée,
canned tomatoes and their liquid.
Stir thoroughly to amalgamate
everything, season with salt and
black pepper, and leave to cook over
very gentle heat for about 30 minutes
or until the meat is cooked.
Heat the oven to 425°F (Gas Mark 7,
220°C).
Meanwhile make the pancakes and
cheese sauce, and butter an oven-proof
dish. When the filling is ready place a
little on each pancake, roll up and
arrange in the buttered dish. Cover
the pancakes with the cheese sauce,
sprinkle over some freshly grated
nutmeg and the Parmesan. Bake for
20-30 minutes or until the top is golden.

Duck

☆ ① ① ① ☒ ☒ ☒

Preparation and cooking time:
2¾ hours
One duck is usually too much for 2
people, so buy a good-sized bird
(about 6 pounds) and divide into 4
portions. 2 portions can be eaten
cold with fresh orange salad, the
others can be reheated and served
with cherry sauce (basic recipe).

1 x 6 lb. oven-ready duck
1 teaspoon salt
2 medium-sized oranges
1 tablespoon finely chopped mint
1 tablespoon vinaigrette
4 sprigs of watercress

Heat the oven to 425°F (Gas Mark 7,
22°C).
Place the duck in a roasting tin and
prick the flesh all over with a
skewer—this allows surplus fat to
run out while cooking. Sprinkle the
bird with salt, but do *not* add any
fat at all.
Roast on the top shelf of the oven for
20 minutes. Then reduce the heat to
350°F (Gas Mark 4, 180°C) and cook
for a further 2¼ hours. During the
cooking drain off some of the fat
from the bottom of the roasting tin
2 or 3 times.
When cooked, remove the duck from
the roasting tin and cut it into
quarters with a very sharp pair of
scissors. Allow to cool, then wrap
each piece loosely in aluminium foil
to keep moist and store in a cool
place.
To prepare the salad, peel the oranges
and remove all the white pith. Slice
the flesh thinly with a sharp knife.
Sprinkle on the chopped mint and
vinaigrette. Unwrap 2 pieces of duck,
decorate with sprigs of watercress,
and serve with the salad.
To reheat the other 2 portions of
duck preheat the oven to 425°F (Gas
Mark 7, 220°C) and cook for 10-15
minutes till crisp. Serve with cherry
sauce (basic recipe), peas and new
potatoes.

Opposite: Cannelloni

WEIGHTWATCHERS' SPREAD

When you are calorie-counting, it is usually boredom and monotony of diet that leads to failure. We all know that eggs, meat and fish provide satisfying protein, but there is a limit to how much steak, omelette and steamed fish one can eat without craving for something more interesting. And it is even worse when you have to apologise for inflicting your tedious diet on another person. So here are 3 very low calorie dishes that will provide interest as well as nutrients—in fact, they are delicious even if you are not dieting.

Poached Trout with Herbs

☆ ① ① ⌧

Preparation and cooking time:
15 minutes

2 large rainbow trout
salt
freshly ground black pepper
2 tablespoons freshly chopped
   parsley
2 bay leaves
1 teaspoon dried thyme
4 slices of lemon
1 tablespoon wine vinegar

Wash and clean the trout, but do not remove the heads.
Place them in a large, deep frying pan. Season with salt and black pepper. Sprinkle on the chopped parsley, bay leaves and thyme. Also add the lemon slices. Pour on 1 tablespoon of wine vinegar and enough cold water just to cover the fish.
Bring to simmering point and simmer for 6 minutes if the trout were fresh, or 10 minutes if they were frozen.

When cooked lift out the fish on a slice and drain on absorbent kitchen paper for a few minutes.
Serve on warmed plates with a mixed side salad.

Steak Tartare

☆ ① ① ① ⌧

Preparation time: *5 minutes*
Here's a delicious, nutritious and slimming dish that requires no cooking at all: both the egg and meat are raw. Use a really fresh egg and best quality steak very finely minced [ground].

1 lb. lean minced [ground] best
   fillet or rump steak
salt
freshly ground black pepper
1 teaspoon olive oil
1 small onion, finely chopped
1 tablespoon capers
1 teaspoon Worcestershire sauce
1 tablespoon finely chopped parsley
1 small egg

Season the steak with plenty of salt and freshly ground pepper. Add the oil, onion, capers and Worcestershire sauce and mix everything very thoroughly.
Separate the egg and mix the white into the meat.
Arrange the steak mixture in a mould

on a large plate and sprinkle with the freshly chopped parsley. Make a small well in the centre and place the egg yolk in it.
Mix the yolk into the steak at the dining table, and serve the tartare with a raw spinach salad.

Piperade Basque

☆ ① ⌧

Preparation and cooking time:
25 minutes

1 medium-sized onion, chopped
a little olive oil
1 small green pepper, chopped
4 medium-sized tomatoes, skinned
   and chopped
salt
freshly ground black pepper
salt
4 large eggs

Fry the onion in very little oil until it is soft—about 10 minutes. Then add the pepper to the pan and continue cooking for a further 6 minutes. Add the tomatoes, season with salt and pepper and heat through.
Pour a little oil into an omelette pan, just enough to moisten it all over the base and sides.
Beat 2 eggs lightly, season with pepper and salt and pour them into the very hot pan.
Put half the onion and pepper mixture into the centre of the eggs, then start to draw the edges towards the middle tipping the remaining egg liquid back to the sides of the pan. When all the liquid has been absorbed fold one edge over, then the other and slide the omelette on to a warmed plate. Keep warm.
Repeat with the other two eggs and remaining onion and pepper mixture.
Serve with a mixed salad.

Opposite top: Piperade Basque; centre: Steak Tartare; bottom: Poached Trout with Herbs

MEALS WITHOUT MEAT

Hazelnut and Tomato Rissoles

☆　①　🗙 🗙

Preparation and cooking time:
35-40 minutes plus 1 hour
Serve these rissoles with a tomato or onion sauce, and accompanied by a green salad—and it will tempt even the most avid of steak fans.

1 tablespoon olive oil
1 medium-sized onion, finely chopped
1 garlic clove crushed
1 lb. tomatoes, skinned
2 teaspoons tomato purée
½ teaspoon dried basil
¼ teaspoon dried thyme
a little grated lemon zest
8 oz. mashed potato
6 oz. [1 cup] hazelnuts, finely chopped
1 tablespoon chopped parsley
salt
freshly ground black pepper
1 egg, beaten
stale white breadcrumbs

Heat the oil in a medium-sized saucepan and gently fry the onion and garlic until the onion is soft and golden. Chop the tomatoes and add them to the pan, together with the tomato purée, herbs and lemon zest. Cook until the mixture is reduced to a thick, jam-like consistency.
Combine the tomato mixture with the mashed potato. Stir in the chopped nuts and parsley. Mix to a fairly stiff but workable consistency. Season with salt and pepper.
Shape the mixture into flat round cakes. (If the mixture is too soft, chill it for 1 hour in the refrigerator first.) Dip the rissoles in beaten egg, and roll them evenly in breadcrumbs.
Heat a pan of deep oil to 375°F (190°C). Deep fry the rissoles for 1-2 minutes or until golden brown. Drain on kitchen paper and serve at once.

Opposite: Vegetable Curry

Cauliflower Cheese

☆　①　🗙

Preparation and cooking time:
20-25 minutes

1 medium-sized cauliflower
salt
1 tablespoon butter
1 tablespoon oil
1 celery stalk, thinly sliced
1 medium-sized onion, chopped
2 tablespoons flour
10 fl. oz. [1¼ cups] milk
1 teaspoon prepared French mustard
4 oz. mature Cheddar cheese
freshly ground black pepper
3 tomatoes

Prepare the cauliflower by cutting off the base of the stem and most of the tough outer leaves. Hollow out the centre stalk, using a potato peeler. Cook the cauliflower for 8-10 minutes in a pan with ½-inch of boiling salted water. Keep the saucepan covered with a well-fitting lid.
Meanwhile prepare the sauce. Heat the butter and oil together in a saucepan and fry the sliced celery over moderate heat for 5 minutes. Add the chopped onion. Cook for a further 5 minutes, or until the vegetables are softened but not browned.
Add the flour, stir and cook for 1-2 minutes then gradually add the milk. Bring the sauce to the boil, stirring, then simmer for 2-3 minutes until it thickens.
Add the mustard and the cheese into the sauce, and season with salt and pepper.
Halve the tomatoes, season and dot with butter. Cook under a hot grill [broiler] until just soft.
Drain the cauliflower and place in a warmed oven-proof dish. Pour the cheese sauce over and surround with tomato halves. Brown the cauliflower cheese for a few minutes under a hot grill [broiler] before serving.

Vegetable Curry

☆　①　🗙

Preparation and cooking time:
55 minutes

This is a moderately hot curry, depending of course on the brand of curry powder or paste you use.

4 oz. carrots, sliced
salt
8 oz. potatoes, diced
1 tablespoon butter
1 tablespoon olive oil
1 celery stalk, sliced
1 medium-sized onion, sliced
1 small cooking apple, peeled cored and diced
3 courgettes [zucchini], sliced
1 tablespoon flour
1 tablespoon curry powder or paste
1 tablespoon tomato purée
½ oz. [2 tablespoons] sultanas or raisins
the juice of half a lemon

Cook the carrots in a pan of boiling salted water for 5 minutes. Add the potatoes, bring back to the boil and simmer for a further 8 minutes. Drain the vegetables, reserving the liquid and keep warm.
Heat the butter and oil together in a medium-sized saucepan. Add the celery, onion, apple and courgettes [zucchini] and fry gently for 5 minutes. Add the flour and curry powder or paste and fry for a further 5 minutes, stirring.
Measure a generous 10 fluid ounces [1¼ cups] of vegetable liquid, pour it on to the curry mixture and add the tomato purée and sultanas or raisins. Bring to the boil, stirring continuously Simmer uncovered for 15 minutes, stirring occasionally.
Add the carrots and potatoes. Cover and cook for a further 15 minutes. Taste and flavour with lemon juice, adding more seasoning if necessary.
Arrange a ring of hot cooked rice on a serving dish. Pile the curry into the centre.

CHEESE FOR TWO

Quite apart from its high nutritional value, cheese has the virtue of nearly always being available in everyone's kitchen. It is therefore ideal in emergencies.

Alpine Eggs

☆   ①   ⊠

Preparation and cooking time:
20 minutes

1½ tablespoons butter
6 oz. [1½ cups] **Cheddar cheese, grated**
4 large eggs
salt
freshly ground black pepper
2 tablespoons butter

Heat the oven to 375°F (Gas Mark 5, 190°C).
Generously butter a shallow fireproof baking dish and arrange half the grated cheese over the bottom.
Carefully break the eggs over the cheese, keeping the yolks whole. Season with salt and freshly ground black pepper. Cover the eggs completely with the rest of the grated cheese and dot with flecks of butter.
Bake in the oven for about 10-15 minutes, until the top is golden-brown and bubbling and the yolks are just firm.

Cheese Scones (biscuits)

☆   ①   ⊠

Preparation and cooking time:
25 minutes
Warm cheese scones, split and spread with lots of creamy butter are perfect for tea on a winter's day.

8 oz. [2 cups] **self-raising flour**
a pinch of salt
a pinch of cayenne pepper
1½ oz. [3 tablespoons] **butter**
4 oz. [1 cup] **Cheddar cheese, finely grated**
5 fl. oz. [⅝ cup] **milk**

Heat the oven to 425°F (Gas Mark 7, 220°C).
Sift the flour and salt into a mixing-bowl, and add a pinch of cayenne pepper. Rub the butter into the flour till the mixture resembles fine bread-crumbs. Mix in the grated cheese. Add enough milk to the mixture to make an elastic dough.
Transfer on to a floured pastry board and roll out to ¾-inch thickness. Cut into rounds with a 2-inch plain cutter. Brush the scones with milk and place on a greased baking tray.
Bake in the oven for 10-15 minutes until golden-brown.

Cheese, Egg and Mushroom Tart

☆   ①   ⊠

Preparation and cooking time:
35-40 minutes

4 oz. **shortcrust pastry**
4 oz. **mushrooms**
2 oz. [4 tablespoons] **butter**
4 large eggs
1 oz. [4 tablespoons] **flour**
10 fl. oz. [1¼ cups] **milk**
3 oz. [¾ cup] **cheese, grated**
salt
freshly ground black pepper
freshly ground nutmeg

Heat the oven to 375°F (Gas Mark 5, 190°C).
Line a 7-inch flan tin with the pastry. Prick the pastry base with a fork, then bake blind for 20 minutes.
Meanwhile, sauté the mushrooms in half an ounce [1 tablespoon] of butter, and boil the eggs for 10 minutes.

Then make the sauce. Melt 1 ounce [2 tablespoons] of butter in a small pan over gentle heat, stir in the flour, then add the milk a little at a time. When the mixture is smooth and thick, stir in 2 ounces [½ cup] of the cheese and season well with salt, pepper and nutmeg. Cook the sauce over gentle heat for 5 minutes.
Remove the tart from the oven and increase the heat to 425°F (Gas Mark 7, 220°C).
Cool the cooked eggs under cold running water, then peel and slice them.
Lay the eggs and mushrooms on the bottom of the pastry case, and pour the sauce over them. Sprinkle the remaining cheese over the top. Cut the remaining butter into flecks and dot over the top.
Return the tart to the oven for 5-6 minutes or until the cheese has melted.
Serve with a fresh green salad.

Coeurs à la Crème

☆   ① ①   ⊠ ⊠ ⊠

Preparation time:
10 minutes plus 8 hours

4 oz. **unsalted cream cheese**
5 fl. oz. [⅝ cup] **sour cream**
1 tablespoon castor [fine] **sugar**
1 large egg white

In a mixing bowl, thoroughly combine the cream cheese, sour cream and sugar, then whisk the egg white till stiff and fold it carefully into the mixture.
Spoon the mixture into individual perforated dishes (or place it on a piece of cheesecloth in a sieve over a bowl) and leave in a cool place overnight to drain thoroughly.
Serve the crèmes topped with fresh raspberries or strawberries. A little fresh cream can be poured over if desired.

Top: Alpine Eggs; Cheese Scones [Biscuits]. Inset: Coeurs à la Crème

A VERY SPECIAL OCCASION

There are special occasions—such as a birthday or your wedding anniversary—when you want to splash out a bit, present a meal that is deliciously out of the ordinary and in keeping with your celebratory mood.

Here is a three-course meal that fills the bill perfectly. You want to look your best and relax together with a pre-dinner drink, so there's no last minute cooking, and two of the dishes are completely prepared well in advance.

Light the candles and enjoy your special evening.

Smoked Salmon and Trout Pâté

☆ ① ① ⊠ ⊠ ⊠

Preparation time:
15 minutes plus 5 hours

This pâté can be made with a great variety of smoked fish (kipper, buckling or smoked eel, for instance) but it is best of all using a mixture of smoked salmon and trout, as here.

Take extra care when setting the table for a special occasion. Flowers, candles, pretty china and linen add a warm, intimate atmosphere.
Many other recipes can be used to good effect besides those given on this page. Shown opposite: Grilled Mackerel with Gooseberry Sauce, and Pears with Chocolate Sauce
Inset: Figs with Pernod

2 oz. smoked salmon (end bits will do)
1 small smoked trout
2 oz. [4 tablespoons] butter
1 teaspoon very finely chopped onion
salt
freshly ground black pepper
a little grated nutmeg

Chop the smoked salmon into very small pieces. Skin the trout and remove the flesh from the bones. Pound the trout flesh and salmon to a pulp and gradually work in the butter until you have a smooth paste. Add the chopped onion and mix thoroughly. Season with salt and pepper to taste and add a little grated nutmeg.
Press the mixture into 2 individual ramekin dishes, cover and chill thoroughly for 3-5 hours.
Serve the pâté garnished with sprigs of watercress, offer lemon quarters to squeeze over the pâté and hot toast to eat with it.

Veal Cutlets baked with Cream and Mushrooms

☆ ① ① ① ⊠ ⊠

Preparation and cooking time:
1 hour 10 minutes
A fairly rich dish that needs only a few boiled new potatoes and a crisp green salad to go with it.

2 veal chops
1 oz. [2 tablespoons] butter
1 teaspoon oil
½ teaspoon dried thyme
salt
freshly ground black pepper
4 oz. mushrooms, sliced
1 tablespoon lemon juice
1 tablespoon flour
2½ fl. oz. double [¼ cup heavy] cream

Heat the oven to 350°F (Gas Mark 4, 180°C).
Gently fry the veal chops in the butter and oil, enough to colour them slightly on both sides. Then place the chops on a large double sheet of aluminium foil in a roasting tin and sprinkle with thyme, salt and pepper. Fry the sliced mushrooms for 1-2 minutes, then add the lemon juice. Sprinkle on the flour and stir well.
Spread the mushroom mixture on to the chops. Pour the cream over and wrap the foil securely round the chops.
Bake in the oven for 1 hour.

Figs with Pernod

☆ ① ① ① ⊠ ⊠ ⊠

Preparation time:
5 minutes, plus at least 3 hours
This is a luxury dessert which is very simple to prepare. The figs look particularly appetizing piled into a cut glass or silver bowl with extra cream in a matching jug.

11 oz. canned figs in syrup
2 tablespoons Pernod
2½ fl. oz. double [¼ cup heavy] cream
1 teaspoon castor [fine] sugar

Tip the figs, together with their syrup, into a serving bowl. Stir in the Pernod, cover the bowl with aluminium foil and chill thoroughly in the refrigerator for at least 3 hours.
Whip the cream lightly with the sugar and serve the figs with the cream on top.

THE UNEXPECTED MEAL

Always be prepared for those embarrassing times when someone important arrives unexpectedly. Your store cupboard (if it's worthy of the name) should be able to cope with at least one complete meal. Below is a three course meal you will be able to rustle up quickly and with a minimum of fuss—and without anyone realizing it is straight off the store cupboard shelf.

French Onion Soup

☆   ①   ⊠

Preparation and cooking time:
20 minutes
This is your first course. It's the cheat's version of Soupe à l'Onion Gratinée (if you're asked) and tastes very authentic. It is always advisable to keep a few canned soups in your cupboard to meet emergencies. And all soups can be jazzed up by the addition of cream, wine or sherry.

1 medium-sized onion, chopped
1 oz. [2 tablespoons] butter
10½ fl. oz. [1¼ cups] canned condensed onion soup
5 fl. oz. [⅝ cup] dry white wine
salt and freshly ground black pepper
2 thick slices of French bread
1½ oz. Emmenthal [⅓ cup Swiss] cheese, grated
2 teaspoons grated Parmesan

Heat the oven to 450°F (Gas Mark 8, 230°C).
Fry the chopped onion in butter until it is soft.
Pour the canned soup and the white wine into a saucepan and heat to simmering point. Add the softened onion and some salt and pepper.
Toast the slices of bread on both sides.

Pour the soup into two oven-proof bowls, add the toasted bread, which should float on top, and sprinkle on the Emmenthal [Swiss cheese]. Place the bowls on a baking sheet in the oven and bake for about 10 minutes, or until the cheese has melted.
Sprinkle with grated Parmesan and serve immediately.

Portuguese Fish Steaks

☆   ① ①   ⊠

Preparation and cooking time:
30 minutes
Here is the main course—a complete store cupboard main course. If you're short of time, you can defrost the cod quickly by placing it (still in the wrapper) in a bowl of hot water.

4 frozen cod steaks, thawed
1 tablespoon flour, seasoned with salt and freshly ground pepper
olive oil
½ teaspoon dried fennel
1 medium-sized onion, chopped
1 garlic clove, crushed
5 oz. canned sweet red peppers, drained and chopped
6½ oz. canned tomatoes, drained

Heat the oven to 400°F (Gas Mark 6, 200°C).
Dry the cod steaks thoroughly with absorbent kitchen paper and cut them into large cubes. Toss them in the seasoned flour.
Heat some oil in a thick bottomed frying pan. Add the cubes of fish and cook until lightly browned.
Then transfer the fish to a lightly buttered casserole and sprinkle over the fennel.
Add the chopped onion and crushed garlic to the frying pan and fry them until pale golden, then add the chopped peppers and tomatoes. Heat them through and season generously with salt and pepper.
Pour the mixture over the fish and

bake, uncovered, for 15 minutes.
Serve wth tinned new potatoes heated through and then tossed in a little melted butter.

Lemon Soufflé Omelette Flambé

☆   ①   ⊠

Preparation and cooking time:
10 minutes
The end to a perfect meal. Most people always have a lemon and a couple of eggs available to make this light and delicious dessert—but it is equally good made with orange.

3 large eggs
1 small lemon
1 tablespoon castor [fine] sugar
1 oz. [2 tablespoons] butter
1 tablespoon brandy

Separate the eggs. Add the juice and grated zest of lemon to the yolks, then add the sugar and whisk until slightly thickened.
Whisk the egg whites until they are stiff and form soft peaks.
Melt the butter in a thick-bottomed frying pan. Pre-heat the grill [broiler].
Carefully fold the egg yolk mixture into the whites then empty the mixture into the frying pan. Stir and fold with a metal spoon for a few seconds to prevent sticking.
Place the pan under the grill [broiler] for a couple of minutes to allow the top of the omelette to brown lightly.
Warm a tablespoon and quickly pour the brandy into it. Set light to the spirit and pour the flaming brandy over the soufflé omelette while you are carrying it to the table.

Opposite: French Onion Soup.
Inset: Lemon Soufflé Omelette Flambé

SUNDAY BRUNCH DANISH STYLE

Cooking a full scale Sunday lunch for two every week can seem extravagant and time consuming. Brunch—half breakfast and half lunch—is a much more versatile meal. But it is important to avoid making it a half-hearted substitute for a proper meal.

Smorrebrod, one of the mouth watering inventions of the Danes, is a colourful and filling answer. Basically Smorrebrod consists of open sandwiches, generously and imaginatively topped with a wide variety of foods. The bread should always be rye (of which there are many types ranging from dark to light) spread thickly with butter. Here is a selection of traditional Danish toppings, which perhaps will inspire you to start inventing some of your own. If necessary use cocktail sticks to secure them.

Salad Shrimp

☆ ☆   ① ①   ⊠

2 slices rye bread, buttered
2 lettuce leaves
2 tablespoons mayonnaise
4 oz. cooked and peeled shrimps
2 twists of lemon
2 sprigs of parsley
a little paprika

Place a lettuce leaf flat on each piece of bread. Place a line of shrimps diagonally across the centre of each slice. Pipe mayonnaise either side of the shrimps and then fill the corners with additional shrimps. Place a twist of lemon in the centre and sprigs of watercress either side. Sprinkle with a little paprika.

The Mariner

☆ ☆   ①   ⊠

2 slices buttered rye bread
6 strips rollmop herring
6 slices of tomato
6 onion rings
2 sprigs parsley

Arrange 3 herring fillets side by side, diagonally on each piece of bread, and tuck a tomato slice in between each herring. Place the onion rings over the top and garnish with a sprig of parsley.

Use your artistic talents to make Danish open sandwiches look attractive and delicious!

The Tivoli

☆ ☆   ①   ⊠

2 slices buttered rye bread
2 lettuce leaves
6 slices of hard boiled egg
8 slices of tomato
1 oz. smoked cod's roe
1 tablespoon mayonnaise

Place a lettuce leaf on each piece of bread. Arrange the egg slices along one edge and the slices of tomato along the other. Pipe the cod's roe in a row of dots down the centre, and top with piped mayonnaise.

Danish Delight

☆ ☆   ①   ⊠

2 slices buttered rye bread
4 small slices cold cooked pork
2 small lettuce leaves
1 tablespoon pickled red cabbage
2 slices of orange (with peel)
2 prunes

Place 2 slices of pork overlapping on each piece of bread. Place a piece of lettuce in one corner and fill it with red cabbage. Place an orange twist in the other corner with a prune.

Hans Anderson

☆ ☆   ① ①   ⊠

2 slices buttered rye bread
2 slices liver pâté
2 small pieces lettuce leaf
4 raw button mushrooms, sliced
2 slices of tomato
2 gherkins
2 bacon slices, crisply fried and drained

Place the slices of pâté on the buttered bread, then in one corner of each piece of bread lay the sliced mushrooms. In the opposite corner lay a tomato slice and a gherkin cut into a fan shape. Arrange the bacon slices diagonally, across the top.

The Copenhagen

☆ ☆   ①   ⊠

2 slices buttered rye bread
6 slices pork luncheon meat
1 tablespoon creamed horseradish
2 slices of orange (with peel)
4 prunes, soaked and stoned
2 sprigs watercress

Fold the slices of luncheon meat into rolls and place 3 side by side on each piece of bread. Spoon the creamed horseradish into the centre of each roll and place a twisted orange slice on top. Arrange a prune on either side, and add a sprig of watercress to one side.

SUNDAY BRUNCH AMERICAN STYLE

Few people are as relaxed about their eating as the Americans, and since Sunday should be a day of relaxation, why not follow their example now and again? The famous 'dips and dunks' for instance are one of the easiest things to eat. Once you've made your dip, all you'll need are lots of dippy foods like potato crisps [chips] salted biscuits [crackers] cocktail sausages and, perhaps nicest of all, long strips of raw vegetables such as carrots.

Guacamole (Mexican Dip)

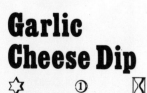

half a ripe avocado pear
2 teaspoons lemon juice
1 garlic clove, crushed
a pinch of chilli powder
a dash of tabasco
1 teaspoon onion, finely minced
1 tablespoon mayonnaise
salt
freshly ground black pepper

Scoop out all the flesh from the avocado and mash it to a pulp with a fork. Add the lemon juice, garlic, chilli powder, tabasco and raw onion. Stir in the mayonnaise and season with salt and pepper. Blend everything together thoroughly. Cover and chill.
(*Note:* it is best not to make this dip more than 3-4 hours in advance because it tends to discolour if left too long.)

Garlic Cheese Dip

1 garlic clove, crushed
2 oz. cream cheese
1 teaspoon minced raw onion
2 teaspoons finely chopped chives
salt
freshly ground black pepper

Blend everything together thoroughly and chill.

The Californian Hamburger

Real American hamburgers, properly made, are every bit as good as an ordinary steak—if not better. If the weather is good, the very best way to cook them is outside over a charcoal grill, but they're none the worse for being cooked under a hot electric or gas grill [broiler].

8 oz. minced [ground] sirloin (80% lean, 20% fat)
salt
freshly ground black pepper
a little oil
2 slices raw onion
2 teaspoons mayonnaise
2 teaspoons relish
2 slices of tomato
4 slices pickled dill cucumber
2 large sesame seed buns

First switch the grill [broiler] to the highest setting—fierce heat is important for initial cooking.
Season the beef with plenty of salt and freshly ground pepper. Divide into 2 portions and shape each one into a round patty about 1-1½ inches thick.
Place on the grill [broiler] pan and brush with a little oil on both sides. Grill [broil] for 1 minute each side then lower the heat and cook for about 5 minutes more on each side for medium cooked—or more or less according to taste.
Toast the sesame buns on the inside. Place the onion rings and 1 teaspoon of mayonnaise on each bun. Then put a hamburger on top, followed by the slice of tomato, the dill cucumber and finally the relish. Top with the other half of the bun and serve.

Hot Chocolate Fudge Sundae

2 portions of vanilla ice-cream
4 oz. plain [semi-sweet] chocolate
1 tablespoon water
½ oz. [1 tablespoon] butter
1 tablespoon toasted almonds
wafer biscuits [cookies]

Heat the oven to 350°F (Gas Mark 4, 180°C).
Break up the chocolate into a heat-proof dish, add the water and place on the lowest shelf of the oven for 12 minutes to melt.
Remove from the oven and beat till smooth, adding the butter. Scoop the ice-cream into sundae glasses, pour over the hot chocolate and sprinkle with toasted almonds.
Serve with wafer biscuits [cookies].

A mixture of textures and tastes can be served at a friendly American-style brunch. Shown opposite: Guacomole and Garlic Cheese Dip, The Californian Hamburger and Hot Chocolate Fudge Sundae

COLD FOOD FOR PICNICS

Below: A pretty country spot on a warm summer's day: ideal for a relaxing picnic. Left: Banana and Walnut Cake

When planning a picnic it is very important to choose the right foods and the right containers in which to transport them. Consider how the meal is to be eaten and carried and bear in mind the season. Wide-necked vacuum flasks now enable you to take ice-creams and sorbets [sherbets] but do remember to put hot foods into a warmed flask and cold food into chilled flasks — this will give both several hours more life.

Picnic Pâté

Preparation and cooking time:
2 hours plus 5 hours
To be at its best the pâté should be made 2 days in advance.

8 oz. pork liver
8 oz. fat belly of pork, rind removed
1 small onion, finely chopped
1 garlic clove, crushed
3 tablespoons brandy
3 tablespoons Madeira
½ teaspoon salt
¼ teaspoon ground allspice
freshly ground black pepper
8 oz. thinly sliced streaky bacon
4 oz. chicken livers, cleaned
1 bayleaf
1 teaspoon powdered gelatine

Heat the oven to 325°F (Gas Mark 3, 170°C).
Coarsely mince [grind] the liver and belly of pork into a bowl. Add the chopped onion, crushed garlic, brandy, Madeira, salt, allspice and pepper to taste. Blend thoroughly with a wooden spoon—the mixture will be rather moist at this stage.
Separate the chicken livers into lobes and stir into the pâté mixture.
Line the base and sides of a 1½-pint loaf tin with the bacon.
Pour the mixture into the lined tin. Cover the top with more bacon slices and lay the bayleaf in the centre. Cover the tin well with a double layer of aluminium foil. Place in a roasting tin and pour in boiling water to come a third of the way up the side of the tin.
Bake in the oven for 1½ hours or until the juices run clear when a skewer is pushed through the centre of the pâté.
Remove the aluminium foil from the

cooked pâté and place a plate and a 2-pound weight on top of the pâté. Leave for 15 minutes then pour off the surplus juices into a bowl. *Sprinkle* the gelatine onto the juices and leave to stand for a few minutes. Then place the bowl in a pan of hot water and stir until the gelatine is completely dissolved. Pour over the pâté and weight it again for 4-5 hours until cold.

Picnic Pie

Preparation and cooking time:
1½ hours
If you have a 7-inch enamel plate on which to bake this pie, so much the better. Line and cover the pie plate in the normal way, and take the pie on your picnic still on the plate, securely wrapped in foil. Alternatively, bake the pie straight on the baking tray as in the recipe then transport it wrapped in foil and tightly sealed inside a plastic bag.

8 oz. back of rib of veal
8 oz. chump end of pork
2 streaky bacon slices, diced
1 small potato, diced
1 small garlic clove, crushed
a pinch of dried thyme
¼ teaspoon ground allspice
½ teaspoon salt
freshly ground black pepper
1 tablespoon stock
2 tablespoons chopped parsley
6 oz. shortcrust pastry
1 egg, beaten

Heat the oven to 400°F (Gas Mark 6, 200°C).
Trim excess fat from the meat and cut the meat into small pieces. Place it in a large bowl and mix in all the remaining ingredients with the exception of the pastry and beaten egg.
Cut off one-third of the pastry and set the rest aside. On a lightly floured surface, roll out the smaller piece of pastry. Using a saucepan lid as a guide, cut out a circle 8 inches in diameter. Place on a baking sheet.
Knead the pastry trimmings lightly into the remaining pastry. Roll out and cut a circle 9 inches in diameter, again using a suitably sized plate or lid as a guide.
Pile the prepared meat mixture onto the smaller pastry round on the baking

sheet, leaving a clear ½-inch border around the edge. Brush the border with beaten egg. Lift the larger pastry round, over a rolling pin, and cover the meat. Pinch the pastry edges together firmly to seal, then decorate. *Knead* and roll out the pastry trimmings and cut into leaf-shapes to decorate the top of the pie. Make a steam hole in the centre and glaze the pie all over with beaten egg.
Bake the pie for 10 minutes then reduce heat to 350°F (Gas Mark 4, 180°C) and bake for a further 65 minutes, or until the pie is golden-brown. Cover the pie with foil if it seems to be browning too much before the end of the cooking time.

Banana and Walnut Cake

Preparation and cooking time:
1 hour 10 minutes
This cake is delicious when served thickly sliced and spread with butter. It also keeps particularly well stored in an airtight tin.

1½ oz. [3 tablespoons] butter
1½ oz. [3 tablespoons] lard
4 oz. castor [½ cup fine] sugar
1 egg, beaten
the grated zest of 1 lemon
the grated zest of 1 orange
8 oz. [2 cups] flour
2 teaspoons baking powder
4 medium-sized bananas
2 oz. [½ cup] shelled walnuts, chopped coarsely

Heat the oven to 350°F (Gas Mark 4, 180°C).
Cream the fats with the sugar and beat until light and fluffy. Beat in the egg and grated zest of orange and lemon. Sift the flour and baking powder together and add to the creamed mixture.
Place the bananas in a small bowl and mash with a fork. Then add to the cake mixture together with the chopped walnuts.
Turn the cake mixture into a buttered 9 x 5 inch loaf tin and level off the top with the back of a spoon. Bake for 50 minutes or until a skewer inserted through the thickest part of the cake comes out clean. Turn out onto a cake rack and allow to cool.

APPETIZERS

On the next two pages you will find a selection of recipes to get your meal off to a delicious start—mousses, salads and a warm soup for a cold day. The main ingredients are fish, cheese and a variety of vegetables.

Smoked Salmon Mousse

☆   ① ① ① ⊠ ⊠

Preparation time:
15 minutes, plus 1 hour
This is a lovely way to make use of those end bits of smoked salmon sold quite cheaply at many delicatessen counters. For a really festive touch you could garnish the mousse most attractively with bands of tiny petit pois and red salmon caviar.

4 oz. smoked salmon pieces
4 tablespoons single [light] cream
1 teaspoon lemon juice
salt
freshly ground black pepper
freshly grated nutmeg
3 tablespoons liquid aspic
1 egg white
5 fl. oz. double [⅝ cup heavy] cream

Chop the smoked salmon coarsely. Put it into a blender, or through a food mill, together with the single [light] cream, lemon juice, a little salt, freshly ground black pepper and nutmeg. Blend it to a smooth purée then beat in 3 tablespoons of liquid aspic.
Whisk the double [heavy] cream until it is soft but firm, then fold it into the salmon mixture. Whisk the egg white until stiff but not dry and add it to the mixture. Taste and season again if necessary.
Pour the mousse into a small deep serving dish or individual ramekins and chill until set.
Serve with brown bread and butter or slices of toast.

Avocado Mousse

☆   ① ① ⊠ ⊠ ⊠

Preparation time:
25 minutes plus 3 hours
This mousse looks as good as it tastes when turned out of its mould and served on a bed of lettuce leaves. Decorate it with paper-thin slices of cucumber, tomato wedges and black olives.

Previous page top: Tuna Stuffed Lemons; left: Greek Island Salad; right: Courgettes [Zucchini] à la Grecque; bottom: Avocado and Seafood Salad

half a chicken stock cube
1 ripe avocado pear
the juice of 1 lemon
½ teaspoon finely chopped chives
½ teaspoon dried tarragon
½ teaspoon onion juice
a dash of tabasco
¼ oz. powdered gelatine
2 tablespoons water
5 fl. oz. double [⅝ cup heavy] cream
salt
freshly ground black pepper

Dissolve the stock cube in 5 fluid ounces [⅝ cup] of boiling water. Peel, stone and dice the avocado roughly. Put the diced avocado into an electric blender together with the stock, lemon juice, herbs, onion juice and tabasco, and blend until smooth, or pass the mixture through a nylon sieve. Pour into a bowl.
Sprinkle the gelatine over 2 tablespoons of water in a cup and leave for 5 minutes. When softened, place the cup in a bowl of hot water and stir until the gelatine is completely dissolved and the liquid is quite clear. When it is cool beat the dissolved gelatine into the avocado mixture.
Whip the cream lightly then fold it into the avocado mixture. Add salt and pepper to taste—the mixture should be highly seasoned.
When the mousse is cold but not set, pour into individual ramekins or one larger mould. Chill until set in the refrigerator.
To turn out the mould, dip into very hot water for a few seconds and invert onto a plate. Serve very cold.

Courgettes (Zucchini) à la Grecque

☆   ①   ⊠ ⊠

Preparation and cooking time:
40 minutes plus 1 hour
Always choose small, even-sized courgettes [zucchini]. Never buy those which look as though they have ambitions to become marrows [large summer squash]. Small courgettes [zucchini] will taste infinitely nicer and look far more attractive when served.

3 tablespoons olive oil
1 medium-sized onion, finely
  chopped

1 garlic clove, crushed
4 tablespoons dry white wine
4 tablespoons water
a bouquet garni
6 coriander seeds
6 black peppercorns
1 small lemon
salt
8-12 oz. small courgettes [zucchini]
2 tablespoons chopped parsley

Heat 2 tablespoons of olive oil in a heavy pan or casserole; add the finely chopped onion and the garlic, and sauté until transparent. Add the wine and water, the bouquet garni, coriander seeds, black peppercorns, lemon juice and salt to taste. Bring to the boil and simmer for 5 minutes.
Trim the ends of the courgettes [zucchini] and wipe the skins clean with a damp cloth. (Do not peel.) Quarter them and cut into 2-inch segments. Add to the simmering sauce and cook over low heat for 20-25 minutes or until tender but still firm.
Transfer the courgettes [zucchini] to a deep serving dish, discard the bouquet garni and pour on the cooking juices. Then allow to cool and chill until ready to serve.
Just before serving, moisten with the remaining olive oil, sprinkle with finely chopped parsley and a little additional lemon juice to taste.

Chilled Seafood Appetizer

☆   ① ① ⊠ ⊠

Preparation and cooking time:
1¼ hours plus 1 hour
Try this salad mixed with a French dressing, as in the recipe below, or alternatively coated with a well-flavoured mayonnaise.

3 oz. [½ cup] long grain rice
2 pints mussels
5 fl. oz. [⅝ cup] dry white wine
4 tablespoons water
1 small onion, finely chopped
2 oz. cooked, peeled shrimps
2 tomatoes, peeled
1 tablespoon chopped parsley
1 tablespoon grated onion
2 tablespoons wine vinegar
4-5 tablespoons olive oil
salt and freshly ground black pepper

Boil the rice in plenty of salted water, until the grains are tender but still firm. Drain thoroughly and set aside to cool.

Meanwhile scrub the mussels well, removing the 'beards' and discarding any shells that do not close. Place the mussels in a pan with the wine, water and finely chopped onion. Cover tightly with a lid and cook over high heat, shaking the pan frequently, until the mussels have all opened—about 5-7 minutes.

Remove the mussels from the pan, shaking back any liquid trapped in the shells. Strain the liquid through cheesecloth or a fine sieve lined with kitchen paper. Rinse out the pan and return the liquid to it. Add the shrimps and cook for 10 minutes.

Meanwhile remove the mussels from their shells, and discard any which have not opened.

Drain the shrimps and combine with the rice and mussels. Slice the tomatoes and add to the mixture, together with the chopped parsley.

Make a French dressing by combining the grated onion, vinegar and oil with a little salt and pepper. Combine all the ingredients thoroughly together with a fork. Pour over the salad and toss lightly. Chill before serving.

Avocado and Seafood Salad

☆　　①①　　☒☒☒

Preparation time:
15 minutes

2 anchovy fillets
2 oz. cooked, peeled prawns or shrimps
2 tablespoons vinaigrette or thick mayonnaise
a little grated lemon zest
salt
freshly ground black pepper
1 ripe avocado pear
a squeeze of lemon juice

Remove all the oil from the anchovies by draining them on kitchen paper. Using a pair of scissors, snip the fillets into small pieces. Place them in a mixing bowl. Add the prawns or shrimps (reserving a few for garnish), mayonnaise or vinaigrette, and lemon zest. Stir to mix and season well.

Cut the avocado in half, remove the stone and peel the skin from the

flesh. Cut the flesh, sprinkle on the lemon juice then add to the other ingredients in the bowl and mix lightly together.

Transfer the salad to a small serving dish and garnish with a whole prawn or shrimp and a twist of lemon.

Greek Island Salad

☆　　①　　☒

Preparation time:
10 minutes

This Greek salad is traditionally made with Fetta cheese. White Stilton is fairly similar, more widely available and perfectly adequate for this recipe.

3 oz. Fetta cheese, or white Stilton
3 large tomatoes, thinly sliced
1 onion, sliced in thin rings
6-8 black olives
1 medium-sized gherkin, sliced
1 teaspoon finely crushed coriander seeds
1 garlic clove, crushed
½ teaspoon oregano
2 tablespoons olive oil
salt
freshly ground black pepper

Cut the cheese into fairly thin strips, about 1½ inches in length. Place the cheese in a salad bowl, add the tomatoes, onions, olives and gherkins and mix together.

In a small bowl combine the crushed coriander, crushed garlic and oregano with the olive oil, and pour over the salad. Season with salt and freshly ground black pepper and serve with hot fresh bread.

Leek and Potato Soup

☆　　①　　☒

Preparation and cooking time:
50 minutes

It seems a pity to make this delicious soup for just 2 portions and it's not so economical. So here we give quantities which will make enough for 2 people for 2 days as a first course, or enough for one complete meal for 2 people with fruit and cheese to follow.

4 large leeks, thoroughly cleaned
2 medium-sized potatoes, diced
1 medium-sized onion, diced
1½ pints [3¾ cups] hot chicken stock
10 fl. oz. [1¼ cups] milk
2 oz. [4 tablespoons] butter
2 teaspoons dried chives
salt and freshly ground black pepper

Cut off the tops of the leeks, leaving the white part and about 1 inch of green. Slice off the root end, split lengthways and slice finely.

Gently melt the butter in a saucepan, tip in the leeks, potatoes and onions and stir to coat evenly with the butter.

Keeping the heat fairly low, place the lid on the saucepan and sweat the vegetables for 10 minutes.

Then pour in the stock and the milk, stir again and season. Replace the lid and leave to simmer very gently for 20-25 minutes or until the vegetables are soft—watch carefully that it does not boil over.

Purée the soup in a blender or press it through a fine sieve. Taste to check seasoning, add the chives, re-heat and serve.

Tuna Stuffed Lemons

☆　　①　　☒

Preparation time:
15 minutes plus 30 minutes

2 large lemons
7 oz. canned tuna fish, drained
2 oz. [4 tablespoons] butter
a pinch of dried thyme
1 teaspoon Dijon mustard
½ teaspoon paprika
salt and freshly ground black pepper
1 egg white
2 bay leaves

First slice the tops off the lemons and set them aside. Slice a little off the other end so the lemons will stand upright. Scoop out all the pulp and place in a sieve resting over a bowl. Press the juice through.

In another bowl mash the drained tuna with the butter, then add the mustard and seasonings. Stir in the lemon juice and finally whip the egg white until stiff and fold it into the mixture.

Taste to check the seasonings, fill the lemons with the mixture, replace caps and decorate each with a bay leaf.

Chill for 30 minutes before serving.

A JOINT OF BEEF FOR THREE MEALS

1. Roast Beef with Roast Potatoes

☆

Preparation and cooking time:
about 2¼ hours
Always allow meat plenty of time to come up to room temperature again if it has been stored in your refrigerator or the butcher's. It is a good idea to rub seasonings into the meat as soon as it comes out of the refrigerator, then leave it at room temperature for 2-3 hours, so that it can lose its chill and absorb the flavours at the same time.

3½ lb. topside [top round] of beef
salt
freshly ground black pepper
2 oz. [4 tablespoons] dripping or
  butter
1-1½ lbs. potatoes

Heat the oven to 425°F (Gas Mark 7, 220°C).
Wipe the joint dry and season with salt and pepper.
Heat the dripping or butter in a roasting tin and brown the joint well all over, over high heat. Set aside.
Peel the potatoes and cut into even-sized pieces. Drain thoroughly on kitchen paper, then turn the potatoes into the hot fat. Season well with salt and freshly ground black pepper. Stand a rack over the potatoes and place the joint on it.
Roast for 15 minutes then reduce the heat to 325°F (Gas Mark 3, 170°C). Calculate the roasting time at 15 minutes per pound for rare meat, 25 minutes for medium and 35 minutes for well done, and roast according to taste. Baste once or twice during the roasting, so that the potatoes absorb some of the juices.
When the meat is cooked to your liking remove the roasting tin from the oven and transfer the joint to a heated serving dish. Keep warm. Turn the oven up again to 425°F (Gas Mark 7, 220°C) and return the tin of potatoes to the oven to crisp. If you are baking a Yorkshire pudding, put it in at this point, near the top of the oven.)

2. Minced Beef Curry

☆ ① ① ⊠

Preparation and cooking time:
40 minutes
Curried food makes a pleasant change —and it's easy, convenient and economical. As with most types of stews and casseroles, a curry actually improves in flavour if kept overnight.

1 oz. [2 tablespoons] butter
1 medium-sized onion, finely
  chopped
1 apple, peeled, cored and chopped
2 tablespoons curry powder, or to
  taste
1 tablespoon flour
1 lb. cooked beef, coarsely minced
10 fl. oz. [1¼ cups] beef stock (or
  thin gravy)
1 tablespoon mango chutney
1 oz. [2 tablespoons] sultanas
  or raisins
1 tablespoon lemon juice
4 oz. [⅔ cups] long-grain rice
salt
4 oz. frozen peas
2 tablespoons sour cream (optional)

Heat 1 tablespoon of the butter in a medium-sized saucepan. Sauté the chopped onion and apple gently for 5 minutes. Stir in the curry powder and cook for a further 2 minutes. Add the flour, cooked minced beef, stock, mango chutney, sultanas or raisins and lemon juice. Bring to the boil, then simmer uncovered for 30 minutes, stirring occasionally to prevent the curry burning on the base of the pan.
About 15 minutes before the end of the cooking time, boil the rice in salted water, adding the frozen peas when the rice is half-cooked. Drain the rice and peas well. Toss with the remaining butter and arrange in a ring around the edge of a warmed serving dish.
Stir the sour cream (if used) into the curry. Taste and season if necessary, then pour the curry into the centre of the rice ring. Serve immediately.

3. Cottage Pie

☆ ① ① ⊠

Preparation and cooking time:
35-40 minutes
The recipe given below calls for packet mashed potato, but you can use 2 pounds of potatoes peeled, boiled and mashed with butter and cream, if you prefer.

1 Spanish [Bermuda] onion, finely
  chopped
2 tablespoons olive oil
1 lb. cooked roast beef, coarsely
  minced
10 fl. oz. [1¼ cups] beef gravy
2 teaspoons Worcestershire sauce
2 tablespoons finely chopped parsley
½ teaspoon mixed herbs
salt
freshly ground black pepper
1 packet instant mashed potato
  (2-3 servings)

Heat the oven to 400°F (Gas Mark 6, 200°C).
Sauté the finely chopped onion in olive oil until soft and golden. Stir in the minced beef, gravy, Worcestershire sauce, chopped parsley and mixed herbs. Taste and season with salt and pepper. Remove the pan from the heat and turn in a deep oven-proof dish.
Make up the instant mashed potato according to instructions on the packet. Spread the mashed potato mixture over the heat in the baking dish.
Bake for 20-25 minutes or until the potato is tinged golden brown.

A JOINT OF LAMB FOR THREE MEALS

1. Roast Lamb with New Potatoes

☆ ① ① ⊠ ⊠

Preparation and cooking time:
about 2¼ hours
Before roasting, make sure you cut away all surplus fat from the surface of the joint to give an even layer of fat approximately ¼-inch thick all round the meat.

1 x 4½ lb. leg of lamb
2 garlic cloves
2½ oz. [5 tablespoons] butter, at room temperature
1 teaspoon dried rosemary
the juice of 1 lemon
salt
freshly ground black pepper
10 fl. oz. [1¼ cups] beef stock
1 tablespoon flour

Heat the oven to 400°F (Gas Mark 6, 200°C).
Wipe the joint clean with a damp cloth. Cut the garlic cloves into about 20 thin slivers. Make enough slits all over the meat to insert the garlic slivers. Mix 4 tablespoons of softened butter with the rosemary, lemon juice, salt and pepper, and spread the butter mixture all over the meat.
Place the meat in a roasting pan and roast according to taste, allowing 23 minutes per pound for very pink, 27 minutes per pound for pink and 30 minutes for well done lamb.
When the meat is cooked to your liking, transfer it to a heated serving dish and keep warm until ready to be carved.
Prepare the gravy by stirring the stock into the roasting pan and scraping the base and sides of the pan as you bring the stock to the boil. Make a paste of the remaining butter and flour, and add in small quantities to the hot stock, stirring constantly. Bring back to the boil and simmer for 2-3 minutes and pour into a heated sauceboat.

2. Deep-fried Lamb Croquettes

☆ ☆ ① ⊠ ⊠ ⊠

Preparation and cooking time:
30 minutes plus 8 hours
This dish is best if the cooked meat mixture is set on a plate, covered and left overnight in the refrigerator. Coat with egg, roll in breadcrumbs and cook the croquettes next day.

1 oz. [2 tablespoons] butter
1 small onion, finely chopped
2 tablespoons flour
10 fl. oz. [1¼ cups] strong stock
12 oz. cooked lamb, coarsely minced
2 tablespoons chopped parsley
½-1 teaspoon Worcestershire sauce
salt
freshly ground black pepper
1 egg
1 tablespoon milk
fresh white breadcrumbs

Heat the butter in a medium-sized saucepan and sauté the chopped onion till soft and golden. Then stir in the flour and cook for 1-2 minutes. Gradually add the stock, stirring all the time. Bring to the boil and cook for 2-3 minutes. Stir in the meat, chopped parsley and Worcestershire sauce. Season with salt and freshly ground black pepper, if necessary.
Remove the pan from the heat. Spread the meat mixture onto a plate. Cover and leave to get cold, preferably overnight in a refrigerator.
When cold and set, divide the meat mixture into 8 equal portions. Roll into neat sausage shapes. In a shallow dish, beat the egg together with the milk. Coat each croquette with egg, then breadcrumbs—twice.
Heat a pan of deep oil to 375°F (190°C).
Deep-fry the croquettes for 2-3 minutes or until golden brown. Drain on kitchen paper and serve immediately accompanied by Courgettes [zucchini] with tomatoes (see Exciting Vegetables).

3. Turkish Lamb Pilaff

☆ ① ⊠

Preparation and cooking time:
30 minutes
This dish is nicest served with sour cream or yogurt. Of course the basic ingredients can be added to or changed to accommodate the leftovers you happen to have available at the time.

4 tablespoons oil
6 oz. [1 cup] long grain rice
2 pints [5 cups] stock
2 tablespoons butter
1 oz. [2 tablespoons] blanched almonds
1 onion, chopped
12 oz. cooked lamb, cut into strips
1 oz. [2 tablespoons] raisins, plumped in boiling water
1-2 teaspoons ground cinnamon (optional)
salt
freshly ground black pepper

In a heavy pan heat 2 tablespoons of oil. Add the rice and cook until it becomes transparent. Pour in the boiling stock and boil over high heat for about 12 minutes. Do not allow the rice to overcook.
Meanwhile, heat 2 tablespoons each of oil and butter in a pan and sauté the almonds in the hot fat until golden. Remove the nuts from the pan using a perforated spoon, and set aside.
Gently fry the chopped onion in the fat left in the pan. When it is soft and transparent add the meat and sauté until lightly browned and well heated through.
When the rice is just cooked, strain and add to the meat pan. Stir in the almonds and raisins and mix lightly with a fork. Season to taste with salt and pepper, cinnamon if used. Allow the pilaff to heat through gently, then serve immediately.

A TURKEY FOR THREE MEALS

1. Roast Stuffed Turkey with Cranberry Sauce

☆ ☆   ① ① ①   ✕ ✕ ✕

Preparation and cooking time:
about 3¼ hours

1 small oven-ready turkey (6-6½ lbs.)
1 oz. [2 tablespoons] **butter**
salt
freshly ground black pepper
For the apricot stuffing:
2 oz. [⅓ cup] **dried apricots, soaked**
   overnight
2 oz. [1 cup] **fresh white breadcrumbs**
¼ teaspoon mixed spice [allspice]
salt and freshly ground black pepper
2 teaspoons lemon juice
1 tablespoon melted butter
1 small egg, beaten
For the chestnut stuffing:
1½ lb. **chestnuts, peeled and skinned**
turkey or chicken stock
   (basic recipe)
1-2 tablespoons butter
salt and freshly ground black pepper
For the cranberry sauce:
8 oz. **cranberries**
5 fl. oz. [⅝ cup] **water**
2-4 oz. [¼-½ cup] **sugar, to taste**
a little dry sherry or dry vermouth

Heat the oven to 450°F (Gas Mark 8, 230°C).
Drain any moisture from the bird and wipe dry, inside and out. Make giblet stock for the gravy. Note the oven-ready weight of the bird.
Then prepare the apricot stuffing. Drain the liquid from the apricots. Chop the fruit and stir in the breadcrumbs, spice, salt, pepper, lemon juice and melted butter. Bind with the beaten egg.
Free the skin from the turkey breast.
Gently push the apricot mixture under the loosened breast skin, pushing down and over the sides of the breast, so that it will keep the meat moist during cooking. Neatly secure the neck skin with skewers.
Next, cook the prepared chestnuts in boiling stock, or salted water, for 20 minutes or until tender. Drain them thoroughly and toss them with butter, salt and freshly ground black

pepper. Stuff the body cavity loosely with the chestnuts, and close the vent with a skewer.
Brush the bird with softened butter and season with salt and freshly ground black pepper. Prick the breast skin all over—this prevents it bursting as the stuffing swells. Then, either wrap the bird loosely in aluminium foil and place in a roasting tin breast down, or put the bird directly onto the rack in the roasting tin, (again breast down) and cover with foil, folding the edges over the lip of the tin.
Roast the bird for 2-2½ hours, turning it halfway through the cooking time. Test by piercing the thickest part of the leg with a skewer: if the juices run clear the bird is cooked. Any pinkness means that additional cooking time is necessary.
While the turkey is cooking, prepare the cranberry sauce. Stew the cranberries in the water until they 'pop', adding more water if necessary. Rub the fruit through a nylon sieve. Sweeten to taste and re-heat, adding a little sherry or dry vermouth if you wish.

2. Turkey Divan

☆   ① ①   ✕

Preparation and cooking time:
45 minutes

12 oz. **cooked turkey, diced**
8-9 oz. **frozen broccoli**
3 tablespoons **grated Parmesan**
1 packet **savoury white sauce mix**
10 fl. oz. [1¼ cups] **milk**
2-3 tablespoons **dry sherry**
2 egg yolks
3 tablespoons **double [heavy]**
   cream
salt and freshly ground black pepper

Heat the oven to 350°F (Gas Mark 4, 180°C).
Cook the broccoli according to the instructions on the packet. Drain thoroughly and arrange in the base of a casserole. Sprinkle with 1 tablespoon of grated Parmesan.
Make up the sauce according to the instructions on the packet, using

the milk. Remove from the heat.
Mix the sherry, egg yolks and cream in a small bowl, then stir them into the white sauce. Add 1 tablespoon of Parmesan. Taste and season the sauce with salt and pepper.
Spoon half the sauce over the broccoli. Arrange the turkey on top and cover with the remaining sauce. Sprinkle the last tablespoon of grated Parmesan on top.
Bake for 30 minutes or until the dish is hot right through and the sauce is bubbling and golden.

3. Turkey in Wine Sauce

☆   ① ①   ✕

Preparation and cooking time:
55 minutes

1 oz. [2 tablespoons] **dripping**
1 oz. [4 tablespoons] **flour**
10 fl. oz. [1¼ cups] **turkey stock**
salt and freshly ground black pepper
1½ oz. [3 tablespoons] **butter**
12 oz. **sliced turkey**
1 small onion, chopped
1 teaspoon dried tarragon
2 tablespoons chopped parsley
2 tablespoons dry red wine
half a lemon

Melt the dripping in a saucepan and stir in the flour. Cook over low heat for about 15-20 minutes until the roux is cooked to a deep golden brown. Gradually add the stock, stirring vigorously all the while to prevent lumps from forming. Bring to the boil and simmer for 2-3 minutes. Taste and season with salt and pepper.
In a frying pan, heat the butter and sauté the sliced turkey until well heated through. Drain the turkey well and place on a heated serving dish and keep warm.
Fry the chopped onion in the fat remaining in the pan. When soft and golden add it to the turkey sauce. Bring the sauce to the boil and add the tarragon, parsley and wine. Taste and flavour with lemon juice, salt and pepper. Pour the sauce over the turkey slices, garnish with lemon and serve.

EXCITING VEGETABLES

There are plenty of legitimate excuses for not cooking complicated or elaborate main dishes every day of the week. But although you may have to resort to quick stand-bys like chops, steaks or grills these can often be made a lot more interesting by serving them with imaginatively cooked vegetables.

Creamed Potatoes with Spring Onions

☆ ① ⋈

Preparation and cooking time: *35 minutes*

12 oz. potatoes
salt
1 bunch spring onions
  [scallions], **cleaned**
1½ oz. [3 tablespoons] butter
1 tablespoon single [light] cream
freshly ground black pepper

Peel and cut the potatoes into even-sized pieces, then cook in boiling salted water for 25-30 minutes.
Meanwhile chop up the spring onions [scallions]. Melt the butter in a saucepan, add the onions and cook for 10-15 minutes until soft.
Drain and mash the potatoes, at the same time adding the spring onions [scallions] and the butter in which they were cooked. Continue to mash until the mixture is smooth and free from lumps. Add the cream and pepper.

Left: Buttered Cauliflower with Nutmeg, Spiced Red Cabbage with Apples, Courgettes [Zucchini] with Tomatoes, Brussels Sprouts with Chestnuts

Brussels Sprouts with Chestnuts

☆ ① ① ① ⊠

Preparation and cooking time:
12 minutes

**8 oz. brussels sprouts, cleaned and
   trimmed**
**3-4 oz. canned, whole,
   unsweetend chestnuts**
1½ oz. [3 tablespoons] butter
freshly ground black pepper

Cook the cleaned brussels sprouts in
boiling salted water for 5-6 minutes
or until cooked but still firm. Drain
well.
Drain the chestnuts, cut them into
halves and sauté in butter for 2-3
minutes.
Add the brussels sprouts to the
chestnuts and continue cooking for 1
minute over low heat, shaking the pan
to coat everything with the butter.
Season with pepper.

Spiced Red Cabbage

☆ ① ⊠ ⊠

Preparation and cooking time:
2 hours 10 minutes
This will provide enough for 2 meals
for 2 people.

1 lb. red cabbage
1 oz. [2 tablespoons] butter
1 small onion, chopped
**8 oz. cooking apples, peeled, cored
   and chopped**
salt and freshly ground black pepper
freshly grated nutmeg
1½ tablespoons water
1½ tablespoons wine vinegar
2 teaspoons brown sugar

Heat the oven to 300°F (Gas Mark 2,
150°C).
Discard the outer leaves of the
cabbage, cut it into quarters and
remove the stalk, wash and shred
finely.

Melt the butter and fry the onions
until softened. Add the apples and
cook for 1-2 minutes.
Into a casserole put first a layer of
cabbage, then a layer of the onion
and apple mixture and season well
with salt, pepper and plenty of
nutmeg. Continue adding alternate
layers until all the vegetables and fruit
are in the casserole.
Add the water, wine vinegar and
brown sugar. Cover with a lid and
cook in the oven for 2 hours.

Courgettes (Zucchini) with Tomatoes

☆ ① ① ⊠

Preparation and cooking time:
25 minutes

8 oz. small courgettes [zucchini]
1 tablespoon olive oil
1 garlic clove, crushed
4 oz. tomatoes, skinned and chopped
salt
freshly ground black pepper

Wipe the courgettes [zucchini] with
a damp cloth and cut them into
rounds about ¼-inch thick. Sauté
them very gently in olive oil for 10-15
minutes, turning them over now and
then, until they are soft. Add the
crushed garlic and chopped
tomatoes and cook for a further 6 or
7 minutes.
Season with salt and freshly ground
black pepper.

Buttered Cauliflower

☆ ① ⊠

Preparation and cooking time:
10-15 minutes

1 small cauliflower
1 bay leaf

freshly grated nutmeg
1 oz. [2 tablespoons] butter
freshly ground black pepper

Wash the cauliflower, cut off the
hard stalk at the base and any tough
outer leaves.
Place the cauliflower upright in a
pan with 1 inch of boiling salted
water. Add the bay leaf and grate
generously with nutmeg all over the
top. Cover the pan with a lid and
simmer for 8-10 minutes or until
the cauliflower is cooked but still
firm (test this with a skewer).
Drain well and melt the butter over
the top. Season with pepper.

New Potatoes with Mint and Chives

☆ ① ⊠

Preparation and cooking time:
30 minutes

12 oz. new potatoes
salt
1 large sprig mint
2 tablespoons butter
2 teaspoons freshly chopped mint
2 teaspoons freshly chopped chives
freshly ground black pepper

Wash the potatoes, but do not peel
them. Place them in a pan, pour
boiling water over them, salt and a
sprig of mint. Cover and cook for
20-25 minutes, or until cooked
through but still firm.
Drain the potatoes. Add the butter,
chopped mint and chives, and shake
the pan to get each potato well
covered with the butter and herbs.
Season with freshly ground pepper.

POULTRY

Roast Stuffed Spring Chicken

☆☆   ①①   ⊠⊠

Preparation and cooking time:
1 hour 40 minutes

1 x 1½ lb. chicken, with giblets
2 tablespoons softened butter
For the stuffing:
2 oz. [1 cup] stale white breadcrumbs
4 tablespoons milk
1 tablespoon butter, at room
  temperature
1 egg, separated
liver from the chicken
2-3 tablespoons fresh dill, finely
  chopped
salt and freshly ground black pepper

Heat the oven to 350°F (Gas Mark 4, 150°C).
Wipe the chicken clean, inside and out. Put the liver aside until needed.
Put the breadcrumbs in a bowl, add the milk and leave to soak for 15 minutes. In a mixing bowl, beat the softened butter and egg yolk.
Chop the chicken liver coarsely. Squeeze the surplus milk from the breadcrumbs, combine with the chicken liver and pass through the fine blade of a mincer [grinder].
Blend the breadcrumb mixture with butter and egg yolk. Then add the finely chopped dill and season well with salt and pepper.
Whisk the egg white until stiff, but not dry and fold into the stuffing.
Loosen the skin all over the breast of the chicken carefully easing your hand between the skin and breast meat. Take care not to tear skin. Push the stuffing between the skin and the breast meat, covering the entire breast with an even, thin layer. Fill the cavity of the bird with any remaining stuffing. Skewer the cavity together, making sure that the stuffing cannot run out from under the breast skin. Truss the chicken.
Melt the butter in a small roasting tin. When it is hot, turn the chicken over in the butter to coat it thoroughly; then lay it breast down on a rack in the tin. Roast the chicken basting frequently for about 1 hour,

until the juices run clear when a skewer is pushed through the thickest part of the leg.
To serve the chicken, remove it from the roasting tin and slice it in half down the middle. Place the 2 halves on a heated serving dish, side by side to reform the original chicken shape.

Duck with Turnips

☆☆   ①①①   ⊠⊠⊠

Preparation and cooking time:
about 2¾ hours

1 lb. young turnips
1 small oven-ready duck
salt
freshly ground black pepper
flour
2 tablespoons butter
2 teaspoons castor [fine] sugar
15 fl. oz. [2 cups] chicken stock
a bouquet garni
1 medium-sized onion, quartered

Peel and quarter the turnips. Place them in a saucepan. Cover with cold water, add salt, then bring to the boil and simmer for 5 minutes. Drain well.
Wipe the duck clean inside and out. Rub all over with salt and pepper and dust with a little flour. In a heavy casserole large enough to take the duck and turnips comfortably, heat the butter. Brown the duck thoroughly on all sides, then lift it out of the casserole and keep warm. Now put the drained turnips into the casserole, sprinkle them with sugar and sauté for 3-4 minutes or until lightly coloured, then lift them out of the casserole and set aside for later use.
Blend 1 tablespoon of flour into the fat left in the casserole, cook for 2-3 minutes, then gradually add the chicken stock, stirring constantly. Bring to the boil, stirring. Add the bouquet garni and quartered onion, and season to taste with salt and pepper.
Return the duck to the casserole and spoon the sauce over the top. Cover tightly and simmer *very* gently for 1½ hours, turning the duck occasionally so that it cooks evenly.
Add the sautéed turnips to the casserole and continue to simmer for a further 30-40 minutes, or until both the duck and turnips are tender.
When cooked, transfer the duck to a

heated serving dish; surround with the turnips and keep hot. Skim the sauce if necessary, then boil briskly for about 12 minutes or until reduced to nearly one-third the original quantity. Strain a little sauce over the duck and turnips and serve the rest in a sauce-boat.

Chicken in Cider

☆   ①①   ⊠⊠

Preparation and cooking time:
1¼ hours

a little oil and butter, for frying
4 small chicken pieces
1 medium-sized onion, chopped
1 garlic clove, crushed
4 slices streaky bacon, chopped
4 oz. mushrooms, sliced
¼ teaspoon dried thyme
salt and freshly ground black pepper
freshly ground black pepper
15 fl. oz. [2 cups] dry cider
1 tablespoon butter
1 tablespoon flour

Melt some oil and butter in a large frying pan and fry the chicken pieces until golden on all sides. Using a perforated spoon, transfer the chicken pieces to an flame-proof casserole.
In the same frying pan (adding a little more oil and butter if necessary) gently fry the onion, garlic and chopped bacon for about 10 minutes. Again using a perforated spoon, arrange them over the chicken pieces in the casserole.
Toss the mushrooms in the frying pan over low heat for a minute or two, then add them to the casserole with the thyme, bay leaf and seasoning.
Pour the cider into the casserole, bring to simmering point on top of the stove, then cover with a lid and simmer very gently for about 45 minutes or until the chicken is tender.
When the chicken is cooked, transfer it to a warmed serving dish with the bacon and vegetables and keep warm.
Work the butter and flour to a smooth paste, then break it up into peanut-sized pieces, add them to the cooking liquid and bring it slowly back to simmering point, by which time the butter and flour will have melted and thickened the sauce.
Taste to check the seasoning, then pour over the chicken. Serve with rice.

Opposite: Chicken in Cider

FROZEN FISH

Marinated Kippers

☆ ① ① ⊠ ⊠ ⊠

Preparation and cooking time:
10 minutes plus 2 weeks or more
After marinating these kippers will
taste as good as smoked salmon.

2 large frozen kippers
   or 4 frozen kipper fillets, thawed
1 Spanish [Bermuda] onion,
   coarsely chopped
10 fl. oz. [1¼ cups] olive oil

Fillet and skin the thawed kippers.
Lay two fillets side by side at the
bottom of a china dish. Cover
with chopped onion and top with the
remaining fillets. Pour on enough
oil to cover the kippers completely,
then cover the dish with a well-
fitting lid.
Leave the dish at the bottom of the
refrigerator for a minimum of 2 weeks,
preferably longer.
When ready to serve, drain the fillets
and serve with thickly sliced brown
bread and butter.

Trout with Almonds

☆ ① ① ⊠

Preparation and cooking time:
20 minutes
Here is another very quick and simple
fish dish. But take care when frying
the almonds—watch them all the time
because they brown very easily.

2 frozen trout, thawed
salt
freshly ground black pepper
a little milk
a little flour
2 oz. [4 tablespoons] butter
2 teaspoons olive oil
4 tablespoons flaked almonds
the juice of half a small lemon
2 tablespoons finely chopped parsley

Season the trout with salt and black
pepper. Dip them in milk, then in
flour, shaking off the excess
afterwards.
In a frying pan melt half the butter
with the olive oil. Fry the fish until
they are golden brown on both sides
and the flesh flakes off easily with a
fork—about 4-5 minutes on each side.
Remove the fish from the pan and
place on a heated serving dish.
Drain the fat from the pan and add
the remaining butter. When it has
melted, add the flaked almonds and
fry, shaking the pan, until the
almonds are golden brown. Sprinkle
with lemon juice and stir in the
chopped parsley. Pour the butter
juices and almonds over the trout
and serve immediately.

Haddock with Prawn and Mushroom Sauce

☆ ① ① ⊠

Preparation and cooking time:
15 minutes
The fact that it is not necessary to
thaw the haddock fillets before
cooking them makes this a
marvellously speedy recipe—about 15
minutes from start to finish.

12-13 oz. frozen haddock fillets
salt
freshly ground black pepper
1 oz. [2 tablespoons] butter
2 teaspoons oil
4 oz. button mushrooms, thinly
   sliced
a squeeze of lemon juice
2 oz. frozen prawns or shrimps
6 tablespoons double [heavy] cream

Season the haddock fillets with salt
and pepper. Melt the butter and oil
in a frying pan. Then fry the fillets

gently in the hot fat, 4-5 minutes on
each side. Transfer the cooked fillets
to a heated serving dish and keep hot
in a low oven.
Add the sliced mushrooms to the
butter remaining in the pan, sprinkle
with a little lemon juice and sauté
gently for about 3 minutes. Add the
prawns or shrimps to the pan and
continue to sauté for about 3 minutes
more, until heated through. Stir in
the cream and simmer very gently
until the sauce is heated through and
slightly thickened.
Taste and add more seasoning or
lemon juice if necessary.
Spoon the sauce over the haddock
fillets. Garnish each fillet with a
slice of lemon, and sprinkle with
finely chopped parsley.

Fried Whitebait

☆ ① ⊠

Preparation and cooking time:
15-20 minutes
This dish is suitable as a fish course,
or as a main dish for lunch or supper.
The *whole* fish is eaten. so do not let
anyone tell you otherwise! It is
important to get the fish absolutely
dry before lightly and singly
flouring each one.

8 oz. whitebait, thawed
seasoned flour
salt
cayenne pepper
sprigs of parsley
wedges of lemon

Rinse the whitebait thoroughly, then
drain well and dry them on absorbent
kitchen paper. Toss the fish gently
in seasoned flour, making sure each
fish is individually and evenly coated.
Shake off any surplus flour.
Heat a pan of deep oil to 370°F
(180°C). Make sure you use a frying
basket with a fine mesh. Fry the
whitebait, a small handful at a time,
for 2-3 minutes until crisply cooked.
Shake the basket from time to time
to keep the fish separate.
Drain the cooked whitebait well,
turning them onto absorbent kitchen
paper; keep hot on a serving dish
until they are all fried.
Serve the fish sprinkled with salt and
cayenne pepper and garnished with
wedges of lemon and sprigs of parsley.

Opposite: Fried Whitebait

FRESH FISH

Sole with Creamy Sauce and Iced Grapes

☆　①①①⊠

Preparation and cooking time:
45 minutes
The grapes in this recipe can be served hot should you prefer. If so, heat them in a little fish stock or white wine just before serving.

1 x 1½ lb. sole
15 fl. oz. [2 cups] water
5 fl. oz. [⅝ cup] dry white wine
3 or 4 black peppercorns
salt
1 small onion, peeled and
　　quartered
1 small bayleaf
a few parsley stalks
1½ tablespoons butter
3 tablespoons flour
2-3 tablespoons double [heavy] cream
paprika
2-3 oz. white grapes, peeled,
　　halved, seeded and chilled

Remove the head from the sole, then skin and fillet the fish. Place the washed head, skin and bones (broken up) in a pan with the water, wine, peppercorns, a little salt, the onion, bayleaf and parsley stalks. Bring slowly to the boil and simmer uncovered for 15-20 minutes or until the liquid is reduced to about 10 fluid ounces [1¼ cups]. Strain the stock.
Season the fillets, then fold each in half, skin side inside. Place in a small greased, flame-proof casserole, pour on the fish stock and poach over low heat for 10-15 minutes. Then strain off the poaching liquid and keep the fillets hot in the covered dish.
Melt the butter in a saucepan and stir in the flour. Cook for a few minutes before adding the strained

Opposite top: Herrings in Oatmeal; below: Grilled Mackerel with Gooseberry Sauce

poaching liquid. Bring the sauce to the boil slowly and simmer for 2-3 minutes, stirring all the time.
Remove the pan from the heat and stir in enough cream to give the sauce a coating consistency. Season to taste. Coat the fillets with the sauce and garnish with a light dusting of paprika.
Serve the sole sprinkled with the chilled grapes.

Herrings in Oatmeal

☆　①　⊠

Preparation and cooking time:
15 minutes
Herrings are never better than when simply prepared, as here—just coated with oatmeal and fried, in the Scottish style. Medium ground or fine oatmeal is traditional, but rolled (porridge) oats can be used if crushed first. Place them in a plastic bag and crush with a rolling pin.

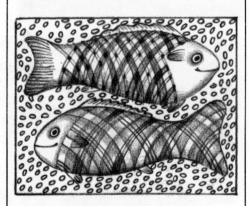

2 medium-sized herrings
3 tablespoons oatmeal
½ teaspoon salt
1 tablespoon butter
1 tablespoon oil
lemon wedges
parsley

Remove the heads from the herrings and scrape the skin from head to tail. to remove the scales. Rinse well and dry with absorbent kitchen paper.
Cut along the underside of each fish, remove the roe and reserve for serving separately. Scrape away and discard the gut.
Open out each fish and place it skin side uppermost on a board. Press along the back of the fish to loosen the back bone. Turn it over and gently ease away the backbone, starting at

the head end. Cut off the fins.
Mix the oatmeal and salt on a large plate and dip in each fish to coat thoroughly on both sides. Melt the butter and oil in a frying pan and fry the herring for 5-8 minutes, turning the fish once half way through the cooking time.
Drain the fish on absorbent kitchen paper and serve immediately on a warmed serving dish with a garnish of lemon wedges and sprigs of parsley.

Grilled Mackerel with Gooseberry Sauce

☆　①　⊠

Preparation and cooking time:
about 30 minutes
This recipe seems to be peculiar to England. It is one of those unlikely-sounding combinations which taste extremely good.

8 oz. young gooseberries
½ oz. [1 tablespoon] butter
sugar, to taste
2 mackerel
lemon juice
salt
freshly ground black pepper
cooking oil

Top and tail the gooseberries. Wash them, then place them in a small saucepan with just enough water to cover. Simmer gently until cooked.
Drain the gooseberries and rub the pulp through a sieve. Mix the gooseberry purée with the butter and sugar to taste. Keep hot in a sauceboat whilst preparing the mackerel.
Pre-heat the grill [broiler].
Gut the mackerel and remove the head and fins. Wash and wipe dry, then season the fish inside and out with lemon juice, salt and pepper. Score each fish lightly on both sides with 2 oblique cuts.
Place on a foil-lined grill [broiler] rack and brush with a little oil.
Grill [broil] under moderate heat until lightly browned. Turn the mackerel, brush with oil and brown on the other side.
Serve the fish immediately they are cooked and accompany with the gooseberry sauce.

Left top: Fresh Lemon Jelly
Bottom: Treacle Tart
Below left: Cream Cup Dessert
Right: Apricot Cinnamon Crumble

DESSERTS

Treacle Tart

☆   ①   ✕

Preparation and cooking time:
30 minutes
There are, in fact, lots of ways of ringing the changes with this old English favourite. For example you could use crushed cornflakes or shredded wheat instead of white breadcrumbs. Then again, you could use orange instead of lemon, sprinkling a little grated zest over the syrup topping for extra flavour.

6 oz. shortcrust pastry
1½ oz. [¾ cup] fresh white
    breadcrumbs
2 teaspoons lemon juice
4 tablespoons golden [light corn]
    syrup

Heat the oven to 425°F (Gas Mark 7, 220°C).
Roll out the pastry to line a 7 or 8-inch oven-proof plate and overlap the rim of the plate by half an inch. Turn the overlapping pastry under to give a double thickness around the rim. Pinch the edges together to decorate.
Sprinkle the breadcrumbs over the pastry followed by lemon juice, then drizzle the syrup on top.
Bake in the centre of the oven for 20-25 minutes until golden brown.
Serve hot or cold with custard or cream.

Lemon Sponge Pudding

☆   ①   ✕ ✕

Preparation and cooking time: *1¼ hours*
This pudding has an apparently disastrous curdled appearance before it goes into the oven. But do not worry: it will separate into a delightful sponge-topped pudding with a delicious lemony sauce underneath.

2 oz. [4 tablespoons] butter, at
    room temperature
4 oz. castor [½ cup fine] sugar
the grated zest and juice of 2 lemons
2 eggs, separated
2 oz. [½ cup] flour, sifted
a pinch of salt
5 fl. oz. [⅝ cup] milk

Heat the oven to 350°F (Gas Mark 4, 180°C).
Cream the butter, sugar and grated lemon zest until light and fluffy. Beat in the egg yolks, then fold in the flour and salt a little at a time alternately with tablespoons of milk. Stir in the lemon juice.
In a separate mixing bowl beat the egg whites until stiff but not dry, then fold into the lemon mixture. Pour the mixture into a small pie dish.
Place the pie dish in a small roasting tin and pour enough water into the tin to come halfway up the side of the pie dish. Bake for 50-60 minutes until the top is well-risen and golden.
Serve immediately, sprinkling the top with a little castor [fine] sugar.

Pineapple Waffles

☆   ①   ✕

Preparation and cooking time:
15-20 minutes
Waffles are very quick and easy to make. That makes them marvellous for an emergency dessert. Heat the pineapple juice from the can to make an accompanying syrup.

3 oz. [¾ cup] flour
a pinch of salt
1½ teaspoons baking powder
1 tablespoon castor [fine] sugar
1 egg, separated
5 fl. oz. [⅝ cup] milk
2 tablespoons melted butter
a few drops of vanilla essence
2 oz. [¼ cup] drained canned
    pineapple, chopped

Sift the flour, salt and baking powder into a mixing bowl and stir in the sugar. Make a well in the centre and add the egg yolk. Mix it in, alternately adding a little milk and melted butter. Then stir in the vanilla essence.
In a separate bowl beat the egg whites until stiff but not dry, and fold lightly into the mixture, together with the chopped pineapple.
Heat the waffle iron and pour a little batter on to it. Cook on both sides for a total of 2-3 minutes. Transfer to a warm serving dish to keep hot while making the rest of the waffles.
Serve as soon as possible with hot pineapple syrup.

Cream Cup Dessert

☆ ☆   ① ①   ✕ ✕ ✕

Preparation time:
15 minutes, plus 5 hours
In this recipe the maceration time given is the absolute minimum. The flavour is improved if the bowl is left covered in a cool place overnight. Don't worry too much about the quality of the wine—one of the cheaper brands of dry white wine from a supermarket will be quite all right.

4 tablespoons dry white wine
1 tablespoon lemon juice
1 teaspoon finely grated lemon
    zest
1½ oz. castor [¼ cup fine] sugar
5 fl. oz. double [⅝ cup heavy]
    cream

Put the wine, lemon juice and zest, and sugar into a bowl. Cover and leave for at least 3 hours.
Pour the cream onto the wine and lemon mixture, then beat until the mixture will hold a shape.
Transfer the mixture to small serving glasses—wine glasses will do—and leave in a cool place for a few hours before serving.

Pears with Chocolate Sauce

☆ ① ① ◻ ◻

Preparation and cooking time:
30 minutes plus 2 hours
Increase the quantities to make a delicious and spectacular party piece.

2 ripe dessert pears
10 fl. oz. [1¼ cups] water
2 oz. castor [¼ cup fine] sugar
1 vanilla pod
2 cloves
For the chocolate sauce:
4 oz. plain [semi-sweet] chocolate,
  broken up into small squares
2 tablespoons of water
½ oz. [1 tablespoon] unsalted butter
1 tablespoon double [heavy] cream

Peel the pears, leaving the stalks on; remove the 'eye' from underneath and slice a little off so that the pears will sit upright.
Place the sugar, water, vanilla and cloves in a small saucepan and dissolve the sugar over low heat, then boil rapidly for 1 minute.
Place the pears upright in the syrup and poach them for 15-20 minutes, then lift them out with a perforated spoon and place on a serving dish. Cool and chill thoroughly.
Just before serving, place the chocolate and water in a small bowl fitted over a pan of simmering water. When the chocolate has melted, add the butter and cream and beat till smooth.
Pour the sauce over the pears and serve at once. Fan-shaped wafers or *langue du chat* biscuits [cookies] make a nice accompaniment.

Fresh Lemon Jelly

☆ ① ◻ ◻ ◻

Preparation and cooking time:
30 minutes plus 2½ hours
We have become so conditioned to shop-bought products nowadays that we forget just what the real thing tastes like (custard, for example, mayonnaise, and tomato soup). Here is a chance to make a real jelly

Left: Pears with Chocolate Sauce

[gelatin] and taste for yourself—then surely you'll never use a commercial jelly [gelatin] again.

3 lemons
1 small piece of cinnamon stick
1 clove
10 fl. oz. [1¼ cups] water
1½ tablespoons powdered gelatine
3 oz. [⅜ cup] sugar, or to taste
a few frosted grapes

Using a potato peeler, remove only the yellow zest from the lemons, discarding all the white pith as this gives a slightly bitter flavour. Put the lemon zest, cinnamon stick, clove and 5 fluid ounces [⅝ cup] of water into a saucepan. Bring slowly to the boil, then remove from the heat, cover and leave to infuse for 10 minutes.
Squeeze the juice from the lemons and strain into a measuring jar (there should be 5 fluid ounces [⅝ cup] of juice—if not, squeeze an additional lemon to make up the amount).
Sprinkle gelatine over the infused water and leave for 5 minutes. Add the sugar and stir until dissolved. Stir in the lemon juice and a further 5 fluid ounces [⅝ cup] of water. Taste, add more sugar if you wish, and stir until quite dissolved. Strain the liquid into a 1¼-1½ pint jelly [gelatin] mould, and leave in a refrigerator or cool place until set.
To turn out the jelly [gelatin], dip the mould for 2 seconds in hot water and invert it onto a plate. Decorate with frosted grapes.

Apricot Cinnamon Crumble

☆ ① ◻

Preparation and cooking time:
55 minutes

6 oz. canned apricots
2 teaspoons soft brown sugar
2 teaspoons ground cinnamon
½ teaspoon ground ginger
For the topping:
1½ oz. [3 tablespoons] butter, at
  room temperature
3 oz. wholemeal [¾ cup wholewheat]
  flour
1 tablespoon rolled oats
2 tablespoons soft brown sugar
1 teaspoon ground cinnamon

Heat the oven to 350°F (Gas Mark 4, 180°C).
Butter a small baking dish and arrange the apricots in it with about one tablespoon of their syrup. Sprinkle them with soft brown sugar, cinnamon and ground ginger.
Then make the topping: rub the butter into the flour and when it is crumbly, mix in the oats and soft brown sugar.
Arrange the crumble mixture lightly over the apricots, sprinkle a teaspoon of cinnamon on top and bake in the oven for 45 minutes or until the top is golden and crispy.
Serve slightly warm with cream.

Caramelized Peaches and Pears

☆ ① ①

Preparation and cooking time:
25 minutes

1 large dessert pear
1 large fresh peach
3 tablespoons demerara [light brown]
  sugar
4 fl. oz. double [½ cup heavy] cream
2 teaspoons castor [fine] sugar

Peel and core the pear, and peel and stone the peach. Cut the fruit into bite-size pieces and arrange in a small shallow oven-proof dish. Cover the fruit completely with the demerara [light brown] sugar and place the dish in the freezing compartment of the refrigerator for 15 minutes.
Pre-heat the grill [broiler] to very hot, then place the dish containing the fruit underneath it until the sugar starts to caramelize. Allow to cool, and if made ahead of time, place the dish in the main body of the refrigerator to chill.
Whip the cream lightly with the castor [fine] sugar and serve with the caramelized fruit.

LEFTOVERS

Very small quantities of leftover meat or vegetables can always be used for light dishes—to fill vol-au-vent or omelettes—and bones will make good stock. Larger quantities can be used to make delicious and substantial dishes as the following recipes prove!

Spiced Mutton Pie

☆   ①   ⊠

Preparation and cooking time:
55 minutes

12 oz. cold mutton or lamb, finely
   chopped
1 medium cooking apple, peeled,
   cored and finely chopped
2 teaspoons castor [fine] sugar
4 pitted prunes, chopped
half a whole nutmeg, freshly grated
4 tablespoons leftover gravy from
   roast lamb
salt
freshly ground black pepper
4 oz. flaky or shortcrust pastry
a little milk

Heat the oven to 400°F (Gas Mark 6, 200°C).
Choose a pie dish that is not too large as the ingredients should come a little above the rim. Grease it with a little butter.
Pack in the meat and apples in alternate layers. Season each layer of meat with salt and pepper, and each layer of apples with freshly grated nutmeg and a sprinkling of castor [fine] sugar. Add a few pieces of prune here and there, and finally pour on the gravy.
Roll out the pastry and cover the pie with it, giving a double layer round the rim. Decorate with the strips left over from the pastry, make a

hole in the centre of the lid, brush the pastry all over with the milk, then bake in the oven for 15 minutes. *Reduce* the temperature to 350°F (Gas Mark 4, 180°C) and bake for a further 30 minutes.
Serve with a green vegetable and redcurrant jelly.

Savoury Meat Pie

☆   ①   ⊠

Preparation and cooking time:
1¼ hours
This is a great pie for using up absolutely all your leftovers! Remember to put all pies onto a baking sheet before they go into the oven as they invariably bubble over during cooking.

4 tablespoons butter
1 small onion, chopped
1 celery stalk, chopped
3 tablespoons flour
15 fl. oz. [2 cups] thin gravy or stock
8 oz. cooked lamb or beef
8 oz. mixed cooked vegetables (e.g.
   peas, beans, carrots, sweetcorn)
2 tablespoons dry red wine
1 teaspoon Worcestershire sauce
½ teaspoon soy sauce
salt
freshly ground black pepper
6 oz. shortcrust or flaky pastry

Heat the oven to 400°F (Gas Mark 6, 200°C).
Heat the butter in a medium-sized saucepan and sauté the onion and celery over moderate heat for 5 minutes. Stir in the flour and continue to cook over low heat until the flour is a deep golden brown. Gradually add the gravy or stock, stirring quickly. Bring to the boil then simmer uncovered for 10 minutes, stirring occasionally to prevent sticking or burning.
Add the meat and vegetables to the pan then stir in the wine, the Worcestershire and soy sauces and season to taste with salt and pepper. Cook for about 5 minutes until amalgamated. Pour the mixture into a 1½-pint pie dish. Cover and leave to cool.
Roll out the pastry to an oblong, 2 inches larger than the top of the pie dish. Cut off a ½-inch wide strip from around the edge of the pastry.

Brush the rim of the pie dish with water and press this pastry strip on to the rim. Brush the pastry strip with water and place the remaining pastry in position over the top of the pie. Lightly press the edges together and trim off the excess pastry. Pinch together to seal well.
Re-roll the pastry trimmings and cut out leaves to decorate the top of the pie. Make a steam hole in the centre. Glaze the pie all over with beaten egg and place on a baking sheet.
Bake for 30-40 minutes until the pie is golden brown on top.

Savoury Croquettes

☆ ☆   ① ①   ⊠ ⊠ ⊠

Preparation and cooking time:
30 minutes plus 8 hours
For this recipe, use any stale bread you have left over to make breadcrumbs; they will keep almost indefinitely in a plastic airtight container in the refrigerator. Please don't use shop-bought breadcrumbs, which are little better than bright orange grit!

2 tablespoons butter
2 tablespoons flour
10 fl. oz. [1¼ cups] plus 2
   tablespoons milk
12 oz. cooked chicken,
   finely chopped
2 oz. cooked ham, chopped finely
2 tablespoons grated Cheddar cheese
2 egg yolks, lightly beaten
salt
freshly ground black pepper
4 oz. [1⅓ cups] fine, stale white
   breadcrumbs
cooking oil or fat for deep frying

Melt the butter in a medium-sized saucepan and stir in the flour. Cook for 2 minutes over moderate heat. then gradually add 10 fluid ounces [1¼ cups] of milk, stirring all the time. Bring slowly to the boil and simmer over low heat for 2-3 minutes, still stirring. Remove the pan from the heat.
Add the chopped chicken and ham, grated Cheddar and lightly beaten egg yolks. Mix well and season to taste

Right: Savoury Meat Pie looks delicious with a beaten egg glaze.
Above: Savoury Croquettes.

with salt and freshly ground black pepper.

Spread the mixture on to a plate. Cover and leave to get cold, preferably overnight in a refrigerator. *When* cold and set, divide the mixture into 8 equal portions. Roll into neat sausage shapes.

Beat the whole egg and 2 tablespoons of milk together in a shallow dish. Dust each croquette with flour, then dip in the beaten egg mixture. Drain well then coat in breadcrumbs.

Heat a pan of fat to 375°F (190°C) and deep-fry the croquettes for about 3 minutes. Drain on absorbent kitchen paper and serve immediately.

Crisp Pancake Rolls

☆ ☆   ①   ◪

Preparation and cooking time:
about 30 minutes
The pancakes can be prepared in advance and stored in layers, between oiled sheets of greaseproof or waxed paper, in a refrigerator. Stored this way they will keep for up to a week. Leftover duck, turkey, partridge or rabbit could equally well be used in place of chicken.

6 pancakes, about 6 inches across (basic recipe)
1 egg
2-3 oz. [⅔-1 cup] fine, stale white breadcrumbs
3 tablespoons butter
3 tablespoons olive oil
For the filling:
1 medium-sized onion, finely chopped
1 tablespoon olive oil
6 oz. cooked chicken meat, coarsely minced
2 tablespoons chopped parsley
¼ teaspoon dried mixed herbs
1 egg yolk
2 tablespoons double [heavy] cream
2 tablespoons milk
salt
freshly ground black pepper

To make the filling, heat the olive oil in a pan and fry the onion until soft and golden. Remove the onion from the pan and mix with the remaining filling ingredients, adding salt and freshly ground black pepper to taste.

Place 2 tablespoons of filling in the

centre of a pancake. Fold two sides of the pancake over the filling and roll up into a neat, secure parcel. Repeat with the remaining pancakes.

Beat the egg with a tablespoon of water in a dish. Add a little seasoning. Coat each pancake with beaten egg mixture then coat with breadcrumbs.

Heat equal quantities of butter and oil in a frying pan and fry the pancake rolls for about 8 minutes or until crisp and golden brown on all sides. Drain well and serve immediately.

Moussaka

☆   ①   ◪ ◪

Preparation and cooking time:
1½ hours

1 large onion, chopped
6 tablespoons olive oil
8 oz. cooked beef or lamb, minced [ground]
4 tablespoons red wine
1 tablespoon tomato purée
1 tablespoon freshly chopped parsley
½ teaspoon ground cinnamon
salt
freshly ground black pepper
2 medium-sized aubergines [eggplants]
1 large egg
10 fl. oz. [1¼ cups] cheese sauce (basic recipe)
a little grated nutmeg

Heat the oven to 350°F (Gas Mark 4, 180°C).
Fry the onion in 1 tablespoon of oil.
In a small bowl mix the wine, tomato purée, parsley, cinnamon, salt and pepper. Pour the mixture into the frying pan and let it cook gently for 10 minutes. Then add the meat and stir until well mixed.
Slice the aubergines [eggplants] into rounds about ½-inch thick, and then into halves, without removing the skins. Fry the slices in the remaining oil until lightly browned; then drain them on absorbent paper.
Into a buttered baking-dish put first a layer of aubergines [eggplants] then a layer of the meat mixture. Continue in this way until all the ingredients are used up.
Whisk the egg. Make up the cheese sauce, add the egg to it and mix together thoroughly. Add a few gratings of nutmeg, then pour the sauce over the meat and aubergines [egg plants] and bake in the oven for

1 hour. When cooked the top will have become fluffy and golden-brown.

Chicken Risotto

☆   ①   ◪

Preparation and cooking time:
50 minutes

5 tablespoons oil
half a green pepper, chopped into small pieces
1 large onion, finely chopped
4 oz. mushrooms
1 chicken liver
8-12 oz. cooked chicken, diced
salt
freshly ground black pepper
4 oz. [⅔ cup] long-grain rice
5 fl. oz. [⅝ cup] hot chicken stock
2 tomatoes, quartered

Heat the oven to 350°F (Gas Mark 4, 180°C).
Heat 4 tablespoons of oil in a frying pan and fry the green pepper, onion, mushroom stalks and chicken liver. Add the diced chicken and season with salt and pepper.
Then add the rice and stir with a wooden spoon so that it absorbs all the juices.
Transfer the mixture to a casserole and pour on the hot stock.
Stir once, cover closely and bake in the oven for 40-45 minutes.
Meanwhile, sauté the mushroom caps and tomatoes in the remaining oil.
When the risotto is ready, serve it garnished with the mushrooms, tomatoes and a sprinkling of parsley.

BASIC RECIPES

Pilau Rice

1 oz. [2 tablespoons] butter
1 small onion, finely chopped
4 oz. [⅔ cup] long grain rice
1 inch cinnamon stick
4 cloves
1¼ teaspoons ground turmeric
¼ teaspoon ground ginger
12 fl. oz. [1½ cups] hot stock
salt and pepper

In a small saucepan melt the butter
over gentle heat and cook the onion
in it for 5 minutes. Next stir in the
rice and the spices.
When everything is well coated with
the butter add the stock and a
seasoning of salt and pepper.
Stir once, bring to the boil, cover
with a lid and simmer very gently for
about 25 minutes or until the rice is
tender and the liquid is absorbed.
Fluff the rice with a fork before serving.

Fresh Tomato Sauce

8 oz. firm ripe tomatoes
1½ tablespoons olive oil
1 small onion, finely chopped
1 very small garlic clove, crushed
¼ teaspoon castor [fine] sugar
½ teaspoon dried basil
salt and pepper

Place the tomatoes in a bowl, pour
boiling water over them and leave for
1-2 minutes. Drain and skin the
tomatoes and roughly chop the flesh.
Cook the onion in the olive oil over
gentle heat for 5 minutes or so, then
add the crushed garlic, finely chopped
tomatoes, sugar, basil and seasonings.
Stir thoroughly, then let the mixture
simmer very gently uncovered for
approximately 25 minutes
When the sauce is cooked, press it
through a fine sieve, reheat and serve.

Pancake Batter

3 oz. [¾ cup] flour
a pinch of salt
1 large egg
5 fl. oz. [⅝ cup] milk
1 tablespoon water
1 tablespoon melted butter

Sift the flour and salt into a bowl,
make a well in the centre and add the
egg. Beat the egg, gradually
incorporating the flour.
When the mixture begins to stiffen
start adding the milk, little by little,
beating all the time.
Finally add the water and whisk
thoroughly till the mixture is smooth
and free of lumps.
The batter can be made in advance,
although it is *not* necessary to let it
stand for any length of time.
Just before cooking the pancakes, stir
in 1 tablespoon of melted butter.

Cheese Sauce

2½ oz. [5 tablespoons] butter
half an onion, finely chopped
1½ oz. [⅓ cup] flour
10 fl. oz. [1¼ cup] milk
3 oz. [¾ cup] grated Cheddar cheese
salt and pepper
a pinch of cayenne

In a small thick based saucepan melt
2 ounces [4 tablespoons] of butter
over gentle heat and cook the onion
in it, without browning, for about 6
minutes, then sprinkle in the flour,
stir till smooth and add the milk, a
little at a time, stirring vigorously
after each addition.
When the milk is all blended into the
sauce add the cheese and a
seasoning of salt, freshly ground
black pepper and a pinch of cayenne.
Arrange a few flecks of butter on the
surface of the sauce, (but do not stir
them into the sauce). Cover with a lid
and leave to cook for 8-10 minutes
over the lowest heat possible.
Just before serving stir in the
remaining amount of butter.

Giblet Stock

the giblets and liver of a chicken,
  turkey or duck
1 small onion, cut in half
1 carrot, sliced in half lengthways
a few parsley stalks
6 black peppercorns
salt to taste
1¼ pints [3 cups] water

Place all the ingredients in a saucepan
and bring to simmering point.
Spoon off any scum that rises to the
surface, then cover with a lid and
simmer very gently for 1½-2 hours.
Strain before using.

Cherry Sauce

4 tablespoons Morello cherry jam
4 tablespoons red wine

Using a wooden spoon, combine the
two ingredients in a small saucepan
and stir over a gentle heat. Bring to
simmering point and simmer very
gently without a lid for 5 minutes.
This can be made ahead and reheated
before serving.
Note: it is important to use Morello
cherry jam and no other variety.

ENTERTAINING

All the recipes in this section are for 2 people, but it is relatively easy to double or treble the quantities to serve 4 or 6 for a party. Here are some suggested menus, but of course you can change them around, or make your own selection from the recipes in this book.

Menus

Entertaining is becoming a lot more relaxed nowadays—and the more relaxed *you* are about the whole thing, the better your party is likely to be. Rule number 1 for entertaining is: don't ever try to overstretch yourself financially or physically. The whole idea of a party is that you and your friends should enjoy each other's company while sharing a meal—so don't cut yourself off from the object of the evening by making things difficult for yourself.

Planning the menu

If you have all day to prepare for a dinner party, have the time, and enjoy boning and stuffing a chicken, well and good. But there is no reason why the cook with limited time—because she has a family of small children or a full time job to cope with—should not be able to give an equally successful party.

In this book you will find many recipes which are ideal for the cook who is short of time. There are first course dishes and desserts which can be made well ahead and served cold, and there are main course dishes which positively gain in flavour if prepared in advance and simply reheated when required.

Seasonal variety and value

The taste and flavour of the food are, of course of primary importance and carefully chosen ingredients are paramount.

Nature automatically provides us each month of the year with a perfectly varied diet—and to be interesting food must be varied. So forget about limp imported salads in winter and outrageously expensive summer brussels sprouts, and get to know when home-grown produce is in season and cheapest.

Search out the very best possible materials and don't be afraid to ask for help and advice. Even if you have to buy eggs, bread and other staple foods from a supermarket, it is well worth finding and making friends with a good butcher, fishmonger and greengrocer.

Attractive presentation

Food must look appetizing too, but that need not involve tomato waterlilies, radish roses, garden peas sitting in nests of mashed potatoes or displays of that sort. Attractive presentation and atmosphere are much more basic, and can turn a simple casserole into an excellent dinner party choice. Simplicity does not, of course, mean lack of style. Attention to detail makes all the difference. A carelessly laid table and a hastily thrown together stew dumped in front of your guests is obviously not condusive to a relaxing and enjoyable evening. However, there's no reason why you shouldn't serve a carefully prepared but simple casserole: if it's presented in a handsome dish it can be most inviting—particularly if you also offer a choice of breads, hot and crusty from the oven, and a selection of ice-cold butters in individual pots (saltless, herb and curry-flavoured butter for example); and follow with a perfectly fresh green mixed salad and a variety of cheeses in peak condition.

The right setting

Experiment with lighting in your dining room—candles can flatter the look of food as well as guests and hostess. Invest in a really nice set of cutlery, glass and china, and add variety with different coloured linen for different occasions. An all-white colour scheme (tablecloth, napkins, flowers and candles) looks cool and elegant in Summer, for example, and deep plum looks warm and welcoming in Winter.

What to drink

If you abide by the generally accepted rule, you won't go far wrong: white wine with white flesh, red wine with red meat. But further than that, try to match flavours. Lamb, for instance is ideally partnered by a light claret while roast beef can stand up to a richer, full-bodied red Burgundy. Quite simply, the more delicately flavoured the dish, the lighter the wine should be.

You may want to serve a different wine to suit each course. In which case the logical sequence is: white before red, dry before sweet, light before full, young before old. In this way a meal would progress from less interesting wines to those with more flavour— the exception being the sweet dessert wines which are always served at the end of a meal.

If you want to take the easy (and expensive) way out, of course, you can't go wrong by serving champagne throughout the meal—unless the food is highly spiced, in which case any wine is wasted, and beer, cider or a jug of ice cold water with a few lemon slices is the perfect answer.

Convenience Foods

Because of the busy lives so many of us lead today, there is a growing trend towards using more and more convenience foods and—as competition between manufacturers grows increasingly stronger—the quality and range of canned, frozen and other ready-to-eat foods is steadily improving.

Frozen items such as pastry, peas and fish; and canned foods like soups, fruits, tuna fish, salmon and anchovies are stocked in every well-managed kitchen today—not only as insurance against emergency situations but increasingly as part of our daily cooking.

As our recipes show, these mass manufactured foods, if cleverly and carefully used, can prove not merely acceptable but suitable for special occasion cooking.

Bachelor cooking

Having some of the work taken out of cooking is encouraging as well as time and labour saving, particularly

for the novice or occasional cook.
A visit to a good delicatessen can be a rewarding experience for the bachelor who claims he would like—but is unable—to prepare a meal for himself.

In addition to offering a wide range of basic and sophisticated store cupboard items—from dried herbs, tubes of tomato paste and mayonnaise, nuts and olives, to exotic canned fruits, vegetables and hors d'oeuvres—he will also find high quality fresh foods (pâtés and smoked fish, salami sausages and other cooked meats, freshly prepared pasta, salads, cheese and coffee)—the wherewithall to produce an excellent meal with minimum work involved whether it be a candlelight occasion or picnic outing.

Picnics

Pastry is excellent for picnics: pies, pasties, quiches and flans.
The time-honoured cold favourites all travel well: lamb cutlets, chicken joints, sliced cold meat, sausages, hard-boiled eggs and cheese. Sandwich fillings should be as moist as possible (for example, tuna fish or cooked chopped chicken should be mixed with mayonnaise and capers); and the fillings should be as thick as one of the slices of bread. Wholemeal and rye bread plus different types of rolls all make a welcome change from plain white sliced bread.
Open sandwiches can be made on the spot, taking butter and a variety of toppings ready prepared in plastic containers. These provide a less stodgy meal than the traditional sandwich and look far more appetizing when combined with salad vegetables. Freshly washed salads and fruits can be drained and packed into airtight containers with tightly fitting lids to keep them crisp and cool.
Also available in the shops are fibreglass insulated packs which will keep foods hot or cold, but any space surrounding the food should be packed with newspaper to prevent loss of temperature. You can also buy sachets for use in the insulated packs; heated in boiling water or frozen in the refrigerator they help to maintain temperature even longer.
Last of all, do not forget to pack cups, plates, knives, forks, spoons, salt, pepper and mustard, sugar and milk in small containers, a can-and-bottle opener—and a damp cloth!

SEASONAL MENUS

Spring

Tuna Stuffed Lemons
Grilled Mackerel with Gooseberry
   Sauce
Apricot Cinnamon Crumble

Avocado Mousse
Spiced Chicken
Caramelized Peaches and Pears

Smoked Salmon Mousse
Duck with Turnips
Treacle Tart

Summer

Salmon Loaf
Chicken in Cider
Fresh Lemon Jelly [Gelatin]

Greek Island Salad
Sole with Cream and Iced Grapes
Lemon Soufflé Omelette Flambé

Guacamole
Poached Trout with Herbs
Coeurs à la Crème

Autumn

Courgettes [Zucchini] à la Grecque
Casserole of Rabbit
Pineapple Waffles

Smoked Fish Pâté
Veal Marengo
Lemon Sponge Pudding

Fried Whitebait
Fruited Partridge
Cream Cup

Winter

French Onion Soup
Duck with Cherry Sauce
Figs in Pernod

Leek, Onion and Potato Soup
Spiced Mutton Pie
Pears in Chocolate Sauce

Avocado and Seafood Salad
Pheasant in Red Wine
Treacle Tart